THIS BOOK IS FOR YOU IF ...

- You write.
- You write to help make sense out of life.
- You write to help uncover the truth about your life.
- You want to use writing to deepen your spiritual awareness.

HOW NOT TO USE THIS BOOK

- Don't hit anyone with it.
- Don't return it to the store.
- Don't lend it to friends; urge them to buy their own copy.

HOW TO USE THIS BOOK

Well, it's a book, so you should read it; but don't just read it: try it out. Writing as a spiritual practice is about writing in such a way as to reveal the fictional nature of self and to sense the factual nature of Self. The exercises we provide are designed to help you do that. So please read our words, but, more important, write your own.

Beyond the Page to
Spiritual Practice

Rami Shapiro and Aaron Shapiro

Walking Together, Finding the Way ®
SKYLIGHT PATHS®
PUBLISHING
Woodstock, Vermont

Writing—The Sacred Art:
Beyond the Page to Spiritual Practice

2012 Quality Paperback Edition, First Printing

Library of Congress Cataloging-in-Publication Data
Shapiro, Rami M.
Writing—the sacred art : beyond the page to spiritual practice / Rami Shapiro and Aaron Shapiro. — Quality pbk. ed.
  p. cm.
Includes bibliographical references (p.   ) and index.
ISBN 978-1-59473-372-7 (alk. paper)
 1. Creative writing—Religious aspects. 2. Authorship—Religious aspects. 3. Spiritual life. I. Shapiro, Aaron. II. Title.
PN171.R45S53 2012
808—dc23

                                                                    2012006011

10 9 8 7 6 5 4 3 2 1

Manufactured in the United States of America

Cover design: Heather Pelham

SkyLight Paths Publishing is creating a place where people of different spiritual traditions come together for challenge and inspiration, a place where we can help each other understand the mystery that lies at the heart of our existence.

SkyLight Paths sees both believers and seekers as a community that increasingly transcends traditional boundaries of religion and denomination—people wanting to learn from each other, *walking together, finding the way.*

SkyLight Paths, "Walking Together, Finding the Way" and colophon are trademarks of LongHill Partners, Inc., registered in the U.S. Patent and Trademark Office.

Walking Together, Finding the Way®
Published by SkyLight Paths Publishing
A Division of LongHill Partners, Inc.
Sunset Farm Offices, Route 4, P.O. Box 237
Woodstock, VT 05091
Tel: (802) 457-4000   Fax: (802) 457-4004
www.skylightpaths.com

CONTENTS

RAMI'S PREFACE

This is a book about writing as a spiritual practice. This is not a book about spiritual writing. Spiritual writing—inspirational writing—has to conform to what the reader finds inspirational. Spiritual writing has to make the reader feel safe, certain, and self-satisfied; it has to leave the reader believing that what she already knows is all that she needs to know. Writing as a spiritual practice is something else entirely. Writing as a spiritual practice has nothing to do with readers per se. You aren't writing to be read; you are writing to be freed. Writing as a spiritual practice is conspiratorial rather than inspirational; it conspires to strip away everything you use to maintain the illusion of certainty, security, and self-identity. Where spiritual writing seeks to bind you all the more tightly to the self you imagine yourself to be, writing as a spiritual practice intends to free you from it. And because it is liberating, writing as a spiritual practice is essentially play.

By play I mean something done for its own sake: it is not about product but about process. Play can be serious and disciplined—think of a great pianist or violinist—but it can't be turned into a commodity. As soon as play is commodified it ceases to be play and becomes work. If you use spiritual practice to go somewhere or get something, you are working rather than playing, and you will fail. There is nowhere to go and nothing to get. There is only what is at this very moment, and no one is keeping you from it except yourself, or rather the self you imagine yourself to be.

I have three rules for writing as a spiritual practice: (1) Don't write what you know; (2) Don't write what you don't know; and (3) Just write.

Don't write what you know.
Writing what you know reveals nothing new. It is simply an exercise in mental recall. Spiritual writing is all about writing what you know, and the fact that nothing new can come from this writing is actually comforting to both writer and reader. After all, with spiritual writing what saves you is the known and the knowable, whereas with writing as a spiritual practice we are dealing with the unknown and unknowable.

Don't write what you don't know.
If you don't know something, how can you write about it? Yes, you can write in order to think through a new idea, but this isn't writing as a spiritual practice. It's a variation of writing what you know or want to know. So you can't write about the unknown, but you can stumble upon it. Which brings me to my third rule:

Just write.
Just put one word after another and see what is revealed. In this you are following the advice of Jesus in the Gospel of Thomas, "Don't cease seeking until you find. When you find you will be troubled. When you're troubled you will marvel. And when you marvel you will reign over all" (logion 2). Substitute "writing" for "seeking" and you begin to understand writing as a spiritual practice.

Don't cease writing. Keep writing no matter what comes up. Eventually you will find something in that writing. At first what you find will be comforting. Throw that stuff away! Keep writing. Eventually you find something that is deeply, disturbingly troubling. That is the good stuff, the stuff you didn't know; the stuff you didn't want to know. And it is this stuff that will free you. When you have no secrets you are free; you reign over all aspects of your life because you are no longer hiding from them or hiding them from others.

But this is not the end. The most troubling and hence potentially liberating discovery is yet to come. What is it? That would be telling, and as every good writer knows, it is better to show than tell.

AARON'S PREFACE

If you read my father's preface and came away feeling a bit raw, let me offer you some salve: this book is not a field of razor blades through which you must walk barefoot. In fact, while our intent is to offer you ways of using writing as a spiritual practice, we have found that the exercises in this book are of benefit to people who just want to write and who are not at all concerned about matters of the spirit.

I come to writing from a rather different place than my father. He says writing can liberate us, and even bring us into contact with the divine. In this, he stands with a long line of philosophers, poets, and writers stretching back to antiquity. So long is this line, and so magnificent and imposing the figures that populate it, that I hesitate to voice even a hint of my own dissent. But there it is. I dissent. Sheepishly, apologetically, with my hat in my hand and my toe twisting in the dirt, I beg to be let off that line.

It's hot and uncomfortable standing there in the dust and the sun, waiting to climb the mountain, waiting for inspiration, waiting to graduate from my flawed humanity and become—as Ralph Waldo Emerson put it—"a transparent eye-ball," seeing all, sensing "the currents of the Universal being" as they "circulate through me."

The sad fact is: I'm not cut out for that kind of thing. I'm a writer. Which means I'm an illusionist. And yet there is a spiritual quality to writing. Writing doesn't *relieve* the symptoms of our flawed humanity; it magnifies them. But it does so in a very strange way.

T. S. Eliot, in his essay "Tradition and the Individual Talent," argues that writing is not an expression of emotion, but "an escape from emotion." Writing creates something new: an "art emotion," i.e., an image of emotion, an illusion of emotion, which exists only in the context of the written work. This is quite different from Wordsworth's "emotion recollected in tranquility." It suggests that, whatever the process of writing entails, whatever it requires, it is less a process of expression than it is of *translation*.

Two weeks ago I was working on a poem. I wasn't sure yet what it was about, though I knew where it was set (the pool at my apartment complex) and what was happening in it (recovering from a biopsy, I struggle with a book by a complicated modernist while watching little kids play in the pool). The poem wasn't working. It had some good lines in it, but it didn't seem to be going anywhere. So, on the advice of another writer—this time a complicated post-modernist—I stuck my poem into something called the Cut Up Machine.

The Cut Up Machine is a program, available for free on the Web (http://languageisavirus.com/cutupmachine.html), that scrambles and recombines texts at random. I plugged my poem in, clicked "Cut It Up," and was stunned to discover that the Cut Up Machine had taken my failed poem and made it into a successful one. It put the beginning at the end, changed the line-breaks, and spliced the stanzas together in ways I hadn't, and probably couldn't, have imagined. But I recognized in this new "Franken-poem" the very emotion I had been trying to get at. It wasn't even an emotion I knew I had; far less one I recollected having. It was something entirely *other* that I nevertheless knew to be my own. This is what my dad might call "writing what you don't know."

This is what writing is for me: discovering something I didn't know. And what writing as a spiritual practice means for me: meeting a self I never was. Briefly. Now, I'm sure that sounds very mystical. Borderline revelatory. So let me caution you, as I caution myself: the revelation is in the words. In the way they fall on the page. What illumination writing may bring is in language, in the tensions created by the system of language. Syntax, diction, rhythm, rhyme, simile, metaphor, metonymy, and so on. That's writing. A *craft*, like carpentry, from which emerges the *artifice* of truth and beauty.

And here is where my father and I come together. We both imagine that in engaging with the craft of writing, we are seeking some kind of encounter: with the human, with the divine, with life, with art, with the other. It doesn't really matter. What matters is that, for us, these encounters occur in words, in the opportunities afforded by ink and paper. The writing prompts in this book are just that: opportunities. They may or may not bring you to an encounter. Some will, some won't. Some will once and then never again. Some won't once and then will some other time. The idea, as Jesus and my father said, is to keep seeking, to keep writing, to keep "turning sentences around" (as Philip Roth says) until one of them turns you around in return.

A NOTE ON COLLABORATION

The text that follows is a work of collaboration. Though in the two prefaces we have written in our own voices and from our own perspectives, we have elected to approach the rest of the book differently. From here on, we will write with a single authorial voice, using the first person. This decision reflects our desire to present a unified and accessible text, but it is also part and parcel of the methodology underlying our approach to writing as a spiritual practice.

You will find, as you read through the following chapters and their accompanying prompts, that we often stress the idea that the act of writing inevitably involves a degree of artifice, especially insofar as writing encourages us to adopt a persona, a self, reflected in the narrative voice. We argue, moreover, that as you recognize the constructed nature of your writing self, you are simultaneously confronted with the constructed nature of your "real" self as well. This confrontation, this encounter with the illusion of selfhood, is liberating, freeing you (whoever this "you" is) to step beyond the all-too comfortable confines of identity, and to encounter whatever lies behind, or beyond, that mask; to encounter the unknown and unknowable.

The collaborative voice we adopt in this book is yet another example of the illusory nature of selfhood. It presents the illusion of a unified "I." But we hope that this is a transparent illusion: one that unsettles itself. The truth is, of course, that the voice you hear while reading is no one's voice; its life is no one's life; it exists only in the progression of words and sentences on the page, and it comes to being only in the encounter between reader and text. Such is the nature of the voice in writing, and such also is the nature of the self, of identity. It is a necessary fiction—one that articulates your whole apprehension of reality—but it is a fiction nonetheless. And as for what may lie beyond it ... who can say?

A NOTE ON STRUCTURE:
THE FIVE WORLDS AND WRITING
AS A SPIRITUAL PRACTICE

E very book needs a spine. I'm not talking about the physical spine that holds its pages, though that too is necessary, but the conceptual frame that holds the ideas together. For this book that spine is the Five Worlds, a model of life that is found in many religions, and that posits the notion that you operate on five distinct though interlinked dimensions or levels of consciousness: body, heart, mind, soul, and spirit. Each dimension has its own way of viewing the world and itself, though it isn't until you get to the dimensions of mind and soul that such talk makes sense.

There are many ways to imagine these five worlds. Some of my teachers speak of them in terms of a matryoshka, a Russian nesting doll. Each doll is in fact a series of dolls with the smaller dolls enclosed in the larger dolls. What I like about this image is that it reminds us that all five dimensions operate in a single system, in this case the largest doll—you. What I don't like about it is the notion that each doll can be separated from the others and lined up next to one another. While this is true of a matryoshka, it isn't true of you. You can't separate body, heart, mind, soul, and spirit into separate selves. They are distinct from one another but not disparate from one another.

I have heard Ken Wilber, one of the great philosophers of our time, offer the a language metaphor for the Five Worlds comparing body, heart, mind, soul, and spirit to letters, words,

sentences, paragraphs, and books or chapters. This is closer to
what I have in mind because moving from one level to another
doesn't negate or drop the previous levels. You can't have
words without letters, or sentences without words, or paragraphs
without sentences, and so on.

What I don't like about this model is that it seems to flow in
only one direction: from lesser to greater, from words to books.
What I envision is a two-way flow from the lesser to the greater
and the greater to the lesser. To share this with you requires an
act of imagination. What I need you to imagine—because I can't
create it for you on two-dimensional paper—is a spiral "biting its
own tail." Not only does the spiral flow up and out—body, heart,
mind, soul, and spirit—but it also flows down and in—spirit,
soul, mind, heart, and body. So when you get to the outermost
edge of the spiral you keep turning and find yourself at the
innermost edge. Like a Möbius strip—the symbol for infinity—
the spiral is never ending, always turning.

When you truly awaken to the reality my five-turn spiral
attempts to represent, you will know that body, heart, mind, and
soul are aspects of spirit. Spirit suffuses the entirety of the reality,
manifesting here as this, and there as that, and here and there as
this and that.

This may not make any sense to you at the moment. That's
fine. *Writing—The Sacred Art* isn't about this spiral, it is about
using the art of writing as a spiritual practice that will awaken you
to this and that as spirit. The spiral is just the spine. So I won't
be exploring these dimensions per se, only offering you a way
of writing that turns you from one dimension to the next. We are
writing to turn the spiral, not to analyze the spiral.

Having said this, however, let me take a moment to quickly
define each turn of the spiral. Body refers to your physical being
and its place in the world. When you use writing as a spiritual
practice to turn the spiral, you begin with a recognition of your
physicality: the breaths you take, the space you occupy. However,

as you write, you will find that you use your awareness of the body to write in a way that turns the spiral beyond the body to the next stage or loop: the heart.

When speaking of the heart, of course, I am speaking in metaphor. What we are really concerned with here is emotion: love and fear, anguish and joy. While emotions arise from the body, and are experienced physically, they operate on a level that transcends the biochemical. Similarly, at the level of heart, writing as a spiritual practice works with emotion even as it leads you beyond emotion.

The next loop in our spiral, mind, refers to the "I" of selfhood. Its foundational perspective is that of the ego, which sees only I and not-I, that which is me and that which isn't me. Mind is all about separation. It makes fine distinctions and recognizes diversity. Yet it often fails to provide a sense of greater unity. Writing to turn the spiral of mind leads you beyond the limited perspective of the ego. It offers you a way to see that while you do have a distinct I, you do not have a separate I. Thus, writing as a spiritual practice leads us beyond the distinction between the one and the many, and toward a realization of the one *as* the many.

This realization is the chief characteristic of soul. Soul is the level of consciousness that sees all things as expressions of the One Thing, call it God, Life, Reality, what have you. If mind is the I that sees itself in contradistinction to all others, then soul is the I that sees itself interconnected with all others. Where mind sees itself as apart from everything outside itself, soul sees itself as a part of everything and doesn't really get caught up in inside and outside. Writing to turn the spiral of soul is writing that takes you to a place of deep intimacy with all life as a manifestation of the one Life. Just don't imagine soul as the real you, the true you, or the eternal you. The real you is what I call spirit, and it isn't *you* at all.

Spirit is the outer edge of the spiral that spirals back into the other four dimensions. There is nothing we say about spirit because spirit isn't an object of observation but the pure Observer itself. If there is nothing to say about spirit, there is no way to write in spirit or as spirit. Writing as a spiritual practice, turning the spiral of spirit, is writing that deconstructs itself, writing that, in a sense, goes beyond writing.

All of this is mere talk, of course, and talking about writing as a spiritual practice is not the same as engaging in that spiritual practice and actually putting words on a page. This book is about doing, and while it is true that I do my best to give you insight into what we are doing, it is the doing that matters most. So let's get on with it.

INTRODUCTION

Spiritual practice isn't about manifesting what you want, avoiding what you don't want, or feeling one way or another about one thing after another. Spiritual practice is about cutting through the illusion of self. As the French poet Arthur Rimbaud put it: "I is someone else." What this means is that you create yourself every day, moment to moment. You weave together stories you invented yesterday with stories you invent today and create this cohesive character called "you" that has no existence outside the stories you spin in the moment that you spin them. But the "you" that is doing the spinning isn't the "you" that is spun.

When you read a book of fiction, you may look for biographical links between the characters and the author, but you don't mistake a novel for an autobiography. Yet when you spin the yarn of yourself, you do just that. You tell stories of the adventures and tragedies of your life, using exactly the same tools as the writer of fiction, but you forget that it is fiction. You imagine—perhaps even insist—that you are the "you" about whom you are talking. Writing as a spiritual practice wakes you up to the story, and at least for a moment gives you a chance to realize who is actually writing it.

To understand more clearly what I am talking about, try the following exercise.

Who's Your Author?

Imagine someone you love dearly, and who loves you in return. Using the first person and the present tense, write about a time when you felt most loved by this person. Recreate the moment in your mind and then describe it on the page as vividly as you can. Do your best to evoke the feelings of that love. Now, write the scene a second time, in the third person, using the past tense.

If you followed along with this prompt, you might have noticed that changing the perspective creates a palpable gap between the "you" writing and the "you" appearing in the scene you wrote. That gap is more obvious in the second version, but the truth is that it is equally present in the first version as well. In both cases, the *narrating* you isn't the "you" who actually feels. There is a "you" on the page flushed with love, and there is a "you" who exists elsewhere and remains untouched.

This second you is a witness, an observer. It is the "you" that resides just behind the "you" you think you are. But do not mistake the witness for the ultimate you. After all, you can become aware of the witness, and that "aware of the witness you" is yet another you.

We can play this game forever, referring back to successive selves as in a hall of mirrors. But as long as there is a "you" in the glass, it isn't the real you. It's only a reflection, an image, an object. You cannot make an object of the real you. The "real you" is the eternal subject; the "I" that knows and cannot be known. This I beholds both actor and witness, though it is neither. This is the I revealed as God in the story of the burning bush (Exodus 3:14), and this is the I Jesus knew himself to be when he said, "Before Abraham was, I am" (John 8:58), and it is this I that we discover ourselves to be when we engage in writing as a spiritual practice.

Most of the time, though, this recognition hovers just out of our reach. We remain trapped within the story we tell of ourselves. Why? Because the story is compelling. Because it works so well as a story that we forget that's all it is.

Consider that among the elements that make a story work is a sense of consistency and coherence in the characters and events. If you write a book about a teenage girl who turns into a vampire in the first chapter, and then suddenly, in chapter two, you refer to her as a middle-aged zombie, you have lost all credibility. Even if your vampire girl is going to become a zombie later in life (something I don't think is actually possible, but it's your story), this has to happen in a logical sequence consistent with the rules of the vampire-zombie universe. Otherwise, the reader cannot accept the story line.

As long as the events of a story appear consistent and coherent, readers will accept them as believable at least within the context of the narrative. When it comes to stories about teenage vampires, this is no big deal, but when it comes to stories about ourselves, it is huge.

My sister, for example, believes that she had a dog named Bowser when we were growing up. No one else in our family—immediate or extended—has any memory of this dog. This fact, however, has not dissuaded my sister from believing in Bowser. Nor has it weakened her capacity to regale us with Bowser stories that only she knows.

Bowser may be a fictional character, but to my sister, and now her children and grandchildren, he is real. What is true of Bowser is true of all our stories: we mix fact with fantasy, imagine links between otherwise disparate events, and weave an autobiography and a worldview that appear coherent and consistent. And *this* we call reality, *this* we call self.

Here is where writing as a spiritual practice comes in, and where it differentiates itself from spiritual writing. The goal of writing as a spiritual practice is to become more and more aware of the fact that reality as we perceive it is a work of fiction, a figment of the imagination. Writing as a spiritual practice is about freeing ourselves from the stories we tell, even as we continue to tell stories. Writing as a spiritual practice is about realizing the I that writes is never the I that is written about. Spiritual writing, on the other hand, is too often just the opposite: creating stories we can hang on to, stories that replace reality, stories that serve the psychological needs of the narrated I while keeping us oblivious to the greater narrating I.

Not all spiritual writing is blatantly narcissistic, and I am not seeking to dismiss an entire genre of writing. I am simply distinguishing between spiritual writing, which is almost always about feeding the self, and writing as a spiritual practice, which is always about starving it.

You starve the self by becoming aware of the storied nature of the self. The more you know that the "you" you know is a fiction, the less attached you are to the story line.

For example, I am a Jew. This is essential to my story. I wouldn't be who I am or do what I do if not for my being a Jew. But what is "being a Jew"? It's a story. Sure, there is a biological element to being a Jew, but there is so much more to being a Jew than biology. This is why people without biological ties to Jews can still become Jews. When you convert to Judaism you take on the Jewish story as your story. Suddenly you were enslaved in Egypt, and you were let out of slavery by God, and you were at Sinai to receive the Ten Commandments, and you have a covenant with God that includes a real estate deal in perpetuity.

A Jew is a person who claims this story as her story. A Catholic is a person who claims the Catholic story as his story. A Muslim is a person who claims the Muslim story, and so on. The same is true of a person who lays claim to being an American or a South African. The same is true of a person who sees herself as bright, capable, and successful. And the same is true of a person who sees himself as dull, boorish, and unsuccessful. We lay claim to an identity and weave the story that comes with that identity into a cloak that covers us from head to foot and from cradle to grave.

You are the stories you tell about yourself. But the storied "you" is not the real you. I wasn't born a Jew. I was born to Jewish parents. This is not the same thing. If my parents had decided to abandon the Jewish story for some other, I would be that other story.

I became a Jew through indoctrination. I was circumcised as a Jew, educated as a Jew, and taught to eat, pray, and love as a Jew. And because I was a Jew I had certain loyalties that I could neither question nor break, and certain enemies that I neither knew nor understood. Because of the story, some foods were edible and others were not; some people were marry-able and others were not; some professions were worthy and others were not.

None of this had anything to do with me—the me that came out of my mother's womb—and everything to do with the me that came out of my parents' imagination. We are the stories we were told, and the stories we tell. Of course, you can break with old stories and adopt or adapt new ones. But who are you without your story? Who are you at the very moment of your emergence from the womb? This "you" is what Zen Buddhists call your original face, your face before your parents were born. When you drop your story, you drop the narrated I of that story, and become who you really are: nobody.

You're nobody. You could become almost anybody, and your parents and society will make sure you are somebody, but the unstoried I is nobody! Writing as a spiritual practice helps you realize this, but not by writing about it. As soon as you write about this unnarrated original face it is just another narrated face, another persona.

The Portuguese poet Fernando Pessoa, working under the pseudonym Ricardo Reis, once wrote: "I feel I am nobody, only a shadow of a face I do not see." In Reis's case this was literally true. He was a persona invented by Pessoa. But he wasn't the only one. Pessoa created and wrote in the names of dozens of alternate personas, the most important of which had their own biographies, their own philosophies, and their own distinct writing styles. So diffuse a personality was Pessoa that he actually had another of his pseudonyms, Alvaro de Campos, write that "Fernando Pessoa, strictly speaking, doesn't exist."

Even when writing in his own name, Pessoa was apt to make this kind of observation. "I do not know how many souls I have," Pessoa said. "Each moment I have changed. Feeling myself always as a stranger.... That's why, like a stranger I read the pages of my being.... I note at the margin of what I read what I thought I felt. Rereading I say: 'Was it I?' God knows, because he wrote it."

Pessoa recognized that the individual self was a fiction, and that, in fact, one's ultimate self could not be identified, and that it might only be experienced as a parade of pseudonyms, a succession of masks. And that behind the parade, beneath the masks, lay the ineffable, the unknowable. The no-thing or no-one or no-body he chose to call God.

Pessoa's writing, then, illustrates the fundamental principle of writing as a spiritual practice: knowing that the self with which you identify is actually a character of your own making allows you to deconstruct it, and in so doing experience a shift from self to Self.

Self with a capital *S* is another way of speaking of God, the unnarrated I. The Self has no story. It cannot be the object of attention. Even though we will be talking about Self, anything I say about it is simply an approximation. As Lao-tzu, the Taoist poet and philosopher wrote millennia ago, "The Tao that can be named is not the Eternal Tao" (*Tao te Ching* 1:1).

The Self, God, the "I" beyond and behind the "I" of story, cannot be named or known. You can no more grasp Self than you can bite your own teeth or smell your own nose. Metaphor is the best we can do when talking about Self: Self is the sky, self is a cloud in the sky; Self is the ocean, self is a wave of the ocean; Self is the sun, self is a ray of sunlight. In other words, Self includes and transcends self. It is not an object separate from self, but neither is it reducible to self.

Writing is a spiritual practice when your intent is to realize that you are Self rather than merely self. This is essentially what Samuel Taylor Coleridge meant when he wrote that the "primary imagination ... [is] the living Power and prime Agent of human perception ... a repetition in the finite mind of the eternal act of creation in the infinite I AM."[1] Which is to say that the act of writing, or any act of high imaginative creation, is an echo of the ongoing act of creation that gives shape to divine being.

However, Coleridge actually makes a distinction between the primary imagination, the secondary imagination, and something he refers to as fancy. If the primary imagination is divine, the secondary imagination is more human, and fancy is merely animal. As Coleridge explains, the primary imagination operates beyond our conscious egoic control; it is the locus of inspiration and insight. The secondary imagination corresponds to egoic consciousness, and does the work of analyzing and rationalizing our experience. Fancy, meanwhile, is passive. It simply accumulates experience and stores it as memory. To approach writing as a spiritual practice, then, means to write with the intention of shifting through these various functions of the mind, much as one shifts gears in a car. To shift from raw memory to rational self-consciousness, and then to go further, shifting from a rational self-consciousness to a suprarational Self-consciousness, from the narrow egoic mind to the spacious mind, the mind in tune with divine creativity.

Paradoxically, having this recognition does not mean losing yourself. Being nobody doesn't mean that you can't have stories. It may be impossible to live story-free. Boring, as well. The difference between the spiritually awake and the spiritually sleeping isn't that the latter dreams while the former doesn't, but that the latter doesn't know she is dreaming while the former does. In other words, the awakened can still enjoy their stories, but they know they are stories. And because they know they are stories, they are free to rewrite them, adapt them to new circumstances, and even exchange them for other stories for the sheer fun of learning new tales.

This is the kind of liberation spirituality brings you. The freedom to be whoever you want without the burden of having to be anyone at all. All this is mere talk, of course. What matters is your experience, and that requires actually writing. Throughout this book, I will offer writing exercises designed to encourage this selfsame recognition: the sudden, fleeting awareness that though your story is you, you are not your story. Through these exercises, I hope to offer you opportunities to encounter what and who you really are: which is to say nothing, which is to say nobody, which is to say God.

CHAPTER ONE

WRITING TO OPEN
THE BODY

Writing as a spiritual practice begins with the body because life begins with the body. We are physical creatures, and we experience the world through our senses: sight, touch, taste, smell, hearing. Writing as a spiritual practice, though it may lead us beyond bodily awareness, nevertheless demands that we recognize the body, grounding our writing and our spirituality in the immediacy of "reality" as it is experienced sensually. In part, therefore, writing to open the body is about writing to become more aware of our bodies and the physical world they inhabit. Simultaneously, it is also about striving to become more aware of the physical properties of language. Indeed, these ideas are related. After all, language is itself rooted in the body, in the movements of lips, tongue, teeth, and throat. And language is inscribed on the body, through the senses of hearing and sight.

A word is a physical object as much as a symbolic one. It takes physical shape and has physical force. In David Lynch's 1984 adaptation of Frank Herbert's science-fiction masterpiece *Dune*, speech sounds, when modulated and enhanced by technology, can crack solid rock, light blazing fires, even explode like bombs. This is metaphor, but it does point to a useful truth: words *exist*, the same way that a leg or an arm or a sperm whale exists. And the physical qualities of speech, of words, can and do affect the way we use and interpret them.

Consider for a moment the difference between a rock and a stone. Both words refer to the same thing: hardened mineral deposits. But we do not use the words rock and stone in the same way. Picturing a rock, we imagine something rough and jagged. But a stone? Stones are smooth, worn; we can skip a stone across a body of water, while a rock will sink straight to the bottom. What accounts for this difference? Part of the answer lies in the sound of the words themselves, in the shape the breath takes as it intones them. For example, say the word *rock* out loud. Listen to the growled "r," the short "ah," and the hard "k." Now say the word *stone* out loud. Listen to its sibilant opening, its full "o" and elongated "n." Now write what you heard. Describe *rock* from the very sound "rock." Describe *stone* from the very sound "stone." Can you hear how the word *rock* "sounds" rough and jagged, while the word *stone* "sounds" worn and smooth?

This recognition of the physicality of words is essential to realizing the emotional power of words. Recently, while teaching a class for beginning writers, I asked my students how they might achieve emotional effects in their writing. In response, they offered ... dead silence. So I asked a different question. "Let's say," I said, "that we're shooting a trailer for a movie. An action movie. We're trying to convince our audience to spend ten dollars to see our action movie on opening weekend. What do we need our audience to feel, and how do we make them feel it?"

This time, I got answers: we need to blow them away; we need their hearts to race; we need them on the edge of their seats, dying to see what happens next. And how do we do it? With fight scenes and chase scenes. With rapid cuts and driving beats. With explosions and gunshots and a deep, male voice growling, "In a world where nothing can be trusted, only one man stands for justice. He is ... the Eliminator."

Or whatever.

The point is that mediums like film and television play on all our senses to move us. Writing does the same. It does it with image, simile, and metaphor. It does it with alliteration and assonance, rhythm and rhyme. It does it with parallel construction and emphatic arrangement. It does it with sentence structure and diction. The Reverend Dr. Martin Luther King Jr. illustrates this beautifully in the following paragraph from his "Letter from Birmingham Jail."

Perhaps it is easy for those who have never felt the stinging darts of segregation to say, "Wait." But when you have seen vicious mobs lynch your mothers and fathers at will and drown your sisters and brothers at whim; when you have seen hate-filled policemen curse, kick and even kill your black brothers and sisters; when you see the vast majority of your twenty million Negro brothers smothering in an airtight cage of poverty in the midst of an affluent society ... when you are humiliated day in and day out by nagging signs reading "white" and "colored" ... when you are harried by day and haunted by night by the fact that you are a Negro, living constantly at tiptoe stance, never quite knowing what to expect next, and are plagued with inner fears and outer resentments; when you are forever fighting a degenerating sense of "nobodiness"—then you will understand why we find it difficult to wait.[1]

This paragraph is remarkably powerful. Much more powerful, in fact, in its unedited state: which is nearly twice as long and contains many more examples of the degradations of segregation. But what is it that makes this paragraph so emotionally resonant?

To begin with, it's the images: the lynch mobs and their innocent victims, the vicious, violent police, inflicting harm on those they should protect, the insulting signs, the "tiptoe stance." These are concrete, physical details that we may visualize, and each brings with it an emotional weight, a sense of fear, frustration, or rage. But there's more going on here than vivid description. There are metaphors—the "stinging darts of segregation," the "airtight cage of poverty"—that bring a concrete, physical reality to abstractions. There is alliteration—"will and whim," "kicking and killing," "forever fighting," "humiliated," "harried" and "haunted"—phrases that, because they ring in the ear, cannot be forgotten.

Then there is structure. The repetitive, parallel clauses that open every sentence: "When you have seen ... when you have seen"; "when you are ... when you are." And the endless run-on sentence composed of fragments that takes up almost the entire paragraph and that cascades horror upon horror until the reader is literally overwhelmed, suffocating and exhausted by the mindless repetitive brutality of it all. A mindless, repetitive brutality that Dr. King has built into the syntax of the sentence itself, for effect, because he knows that words are things, shapes in the air, that can soothe and calm, that can electrify, terrify, and inflame.

So, part of writing from the body is writing with an awareness of the way language appeals to our senses. We must cultivate an awareness of the sonic and imagistic qualities of language, an awareness of the poetic and structural devices that enable words to become gestures. Let's pause here a moment to practice cultivating that awareness by working through a few prompts.

Projective Verse

One way to write from the body is to ground your writing in your breathing. This exercise is based on the poet Charles Olson's suggestion that poets vary the length of poetic lines according to the length of the poet's breath.

A few brief notes, though, before we begin. First, for this prompt you may write about anything: the space around you, the sensation of breathing itself, the events of your day, a memory—anything. Whatever moves you in the moment. Second, punctuation interposes the rhythms of English grammar into writing. So, because this prompt asks us to allow our breathing to dictate the rhythm of our writing, it may be easier to accomplish if you write without punctuation. Finally, breathe naturally. Let the writing follow your breath rather than trying to force your breath to follow the writing. With these caveats in place, let's move on to the prompt.

1. Take a deep, slow breath: as deep and slow as you can.
2. Exhale, slowly and deliberately.
3. As you exhale, clear your mind. Imagine that the breath is cleansing you of everything that has happened to you today.
4. Continue breathing deeply and slowly until you relax.
5. When you sense you are ready, begin writing on an exhaled breath.
6. Continue writing until you have finished exhaling, then, when it is time to inhale, pause until you are ready to exhale again.
7. When you exhale, begin writing again on a new line.
8. Continue breathing naturally, pausing when you inhale and writing when you exhale, beginning a new line with each exhalation. Keep breathing and writing as long as you feel comfortable.

The first time you attempt this prompt, it is likely to feel extremely unnatural. That's OK. You don't have to write like this all the time. The goal is simply to experiment, to see what happens when we allow writing to flow with our breath. Practice this prompt on and off as you see fit, and each time you complete the prompt, try spending some time reflecting on the experience. How did it feel to write this way? What effects did this experiment have on your writing? How did it affect your thought processes?

Soundings

There are any number of ways to experiment with using sound in writing, and to begin to build a more keen awareness of the role of sonic effects in writing. What follows is a prompt that helps you develop your writing ear by playing with phonemes, units of sound equivalent to a single syllable. By isolating phonemes, we become more attuned to the sonic building blocks of language, and more attuned to the inherent musicality of language. This prompt asks you to use phonemes to help you identify sonic relationships between words, and to work with those relationships in your writing.

1. Choose a word that you enjoy for purely sonic reasons. Any word that tickles your ear will do.
2. Isolate one or two phonemes in that word. Try to choose the phonemes you feel are essential to the aesthetic effect of the word.
3. Using the phonemes you selected, create a list of words that contain related sounds. Don't worry about making them match exactly. Slight variations are perfectly acceptable.
4. Write a sentence, a paragraph, and/or a poem containing as many of the words in your list words as you can.

For example, I like the word *ruffle*. Something about the *uffle* sound makes me laugh. So, I might use *uffle* as my phoneme, or I might break it down further and look for words that contain either the *uff* phoneme or the *full* phoneme. Off the top of my head, I might create the following list from all three sounds: *scuffle, kerfuffle, muffle, shovel, tussle, rustle, bubble, full, bull, toll, roll, shoal, scold, mold, fold, rough, tough, fluff, stuff, muff, shove*. Now that I have my list, my next challenge is to try to get as many of these words as possible into a piece of coherent, or semi-coherent, writing:

> I breathe rough: a rustle in each lung-full
> of air, muffled but audible, like the scuffle
> of a pillow fight, the slight kerfuffle
> of impact as feathers tussle.

Obviously, this is not a complete poem. It's barely a stanza. But so what? It is sonically interesting (at least to me), playing with a whole set of phoneme pairings, some of which—*muffle* and *audible*, for example—were not even on my list, and others of which—*fight, slight*—were simply incidental. And yet there they are. And this is the point: in writing my little stanza I began to hear the words in a very specific way, sensing how they fit together, how they echoed each other. My ear guided my writing, and that awareness of the physical, gestural qualities of words is precisely what this prompt is meant to engender.

Whether I continue working with this poem or not, the experience of writing it, and of continuing to play with sound for sound's sake, will certainly effect my approach to writing in the future. And this is the case for all of us. By honing our awareness of the sounds of words in exercises like this one, we may eventually come to write, or so we hope, with our ears wide open.

WRITING TO ENGAGE THE WORLD

The above prompts focus primarily on engaging the physicality of language by playing with its sounds. But of course, as I said earlier, we must also cultivate an awareness of the imagistic qualities of language, its ability to represent the world using vivid, concrete images.

When we looked at "Letter from Birmingham Jail," we saw that Martin Luther King doesn't just tell his readers about the evils of segregation; he shows them: through concrete narrative examples (the lynch mobs, the policemen, the signs), through simile and metaphor ("the stinging darts of segregation"). What Dr. King knows that we, as writers, would do well to remember is that human intellect, human consciousness, is ultimately based in the sensory apparatus of our bodies. Sure, language allows us to conceptualize abstractions, like art or beauty or God, and we should not ignore the importance of that function. But the primal power of language resides most fully in its ability to represent, or better, to conjure up, *things*.

There is an important corollary to this point in terms of writing practice that emerges in the work of the German poet Rainer Maria Rilke. Rilke tells us to "come close to nature" and to "write about what your everyday life offers you ... [using] the things around you, the images from your dreams, and the objects you remember."[2] Rilke is saying that we must use our writing to engage with the world, rather than to escape from it, or to comment on it. Our writing must investigate the material realities, the objects, of everyday life, whether they be carousels or panthers.

Rilke's own poetry is full of poems about objects. In fact, he coined a word for these poems: the *Dinggedicht*, or "thing poem." "Thing poems" do not comment on the world, they simply observe it acutely, allowing the relationships between one thing and another to take on significance however they will, without forcing and without comment. This practice of representation without commentary is essential to writing as a spiritual practice because it short-circuits our penchant for narrative, for explaining the world in terms of intellectual abstractions, demanding instead that we observe the world intensely, building our understanding of life on our observations, rather than imposing some made-up narrative or thematic frame.

Dinggedicht

One way to engage the world this way is to take a page from Rilke's book and write a *Dinggedicht* of your own. As I explained, the *Dinggedicht* is ostensibly a poem of the physical world. However, the *Dinggedicht* does not merely describe the physical world. It enters the physical world in order to ask it what it wants to say. So while the *Dinggedicht* treats the world objectively, with the eye of the scientist recording detail, it also aims to reach such a pitch of intense observation that, through the poem, the writer enters into a dialogue with the object under scrutiny that allows the object to speak for itself, revealing the essence of its existence.

To write a *Dinggedicht*, you must first select an object, then observe it, and finally describe it in a way that allows the thing to speak for itself. This means, of course, that you cannot impose your own ideas on the object you are writing about. You can only observe it and describe it, focusing on the concrete. Don't tell me that the steeple symbolizes our aspirations to holiness; tell me it is like two hands clasped in prayer. What you will find as you practice this type of writing is that your awareness of the world changes. You will no longer impose a metaphysical framework, or metaphorical understanding, on the world. You will discover such visions in the shape of things as they really are. This is the challenge of the *Dinggedicht*: to write in such a way that the world speaks for itself.

Here are a few guiding principles for writing a *Dinggedicht*:

- Select an object that fascinates you.
- Describe the object in terms of only a few key attributes, its color, its movement, etc.
- Keep your language simple. Use primarily concrete nouns and verbs, especially nouns and verbs particular to the object you are describing.

- Resist the urge to editorialize, or to create complex metaphors. Keep your focus on the object.
- When metaphor or simile arises, keep comparisons concrete. That is, compare objects to other objects.

Haiku

Another way to enter this world-centric writing is through Japanese haiku. Although many haiku include the self, the narrative I, here are three examples that do not:

> Ancient sleepy pool.
> A frog unexpectedly
> Hops in. Ker-plop!
> (Basho)
> *
>
> Over the mountain,
> The full white moon smiles brightly
> On the flower thief.
> (Issa)
> *
>
> Fearless dragon-fly
> Resting on the flyswatter,
> Prepare to die!
> (Kohyo)

Traditional haiku follows a strict syllabic pattern, 5-7-5, but as my translations make clear, the pattern is not my concern. What matters to us in the context of writing as spiritual practice is the complete absence of a storied I. Compare these haiku with the opening of Robert Frost's poem "The Road Not Taken":

> Two roads diverged in a yellow wood,
> And sorry I could not travel both
> And be one traveler, long I stood

And looked down one as far as I could
To where it bent in the undergrowth;[3]

Is this about the road or the traveler; about the seen or the seer? Imagine rewriting Frost's poem as haiku:

A yellow wood
Two roads diverged
One lost in undergrowth.

This is writing to open the body, writing as spiritual practice. It is language stripped of the narrative I's temptation to impose meaning on what it sees, writing that meets the world as directly as possible, and—because it does so— is open to discovering the world anew, apprehending the meanings that arise from the truth of things as they are.

Zang Tumb Tuuum

I lifted the bizarre name for this prompt from its inventor, the Italian Futurist writer Filippo Tomaso Marinetti. "Zang Tumb Tuuum" is the title of an experimental, concrete sound poem written by Marinetti to describe, or rather reproduce, his experience as a war correspondent during the Bulgarian-Serbian siege of 1912–13. The poem engages, Marinetti explains, in an extended language game designed to "destroy the I in literature" and "replace him with Matter." The idea is to write in such a way as to remove every trace of human consciousness from our writing, and thus to excise all history, all psychology, all wisdom, and all logic from our representation of experience.

Why? Because the human psyche demands that the world make sense in human terms, and in doing so it twists nature and life out of shape, forcing them to conform to human ideas and ideologies. In a Zang Tumb

Tuuum, we free ourselves from ideas and ideologies. We free ourselves from having to make sense, and free ourselves simply to sense, recording the language of things as they happen around us. Here are the rules of Zang Tumb Tuuum:

1. Break the rules of syntax; reverse verbs and subjects, subjects and objects.
2. Do not write in complete sentences.
3. Replace punctuation with white spaces of various sizes.
4. Avoid adjectives and adverbs.
5. Use verbs only in unconjugated form: be, run, do, sit, etc.
6. Link nouns via dashes or in descriptive compounds, such as *bloodymud*.
7. Embrace onomatopoeia: write down sounds as they sound, not with the words: dogs don't bark, they ...?
8. Write quickly, in immediate response to your senses.

Zang Tumb Tuuum works very well in loud and chaotic settings: a video game arcade, a construction site, on the side of a freeway, at a daycare center, or in the cafeteria at your local mall. But it will still work, and just as well, at the beach, in your home or office, in the woods, or wherever. It will also work if you are writing from memory or from imagination. I would suggest you try all of these methods.

Take a pen and notebook, or your laptop, to your kid's Little League game, or to a tailgate party, and spend ten to fifteen minutes writing, recording your impressions according to Marinetti's rules. Or take your notebook to your favorite park and record what you experience there. Or close your eyes and remember making love, and record that. Wherever you choose to write, and whatever you choose to write about, give yourself at least ten to fifteen minutes (or longer if you find yourself falling into a rhythm) and stick with the rules of the game. Remember: the key to writing in this fashion is not necessarily to overload your senses with immediate stimulation but rather to overload your writing with immediate sensory detail. In this way, we turn our perspective from "comprehension" to "apprehension," from the understanding of life crafted by self, to the experience of life lived by the body. Good Zanging!

Where Are You?

This final image-based prompt asks you to take the sensual awareness you have been working with in the previous two prompts and apply it to your own immediate environment as a way of grounding yourself and your writing process in the here and now.

Using vivid, concrete detail, describe the place where you are at this very moment. Include everything: the position of your body, the feel of your skin, the color of the sky or the texture of the carpet, the temperature of the air, the ambient noise level, everything. As you write, allow yourself to respond to each element of your environment as it presents itself to your attention, but don't stay too long with any given detail. Let the description flow along at its own pace, and let your thoughts fall into and out of focus where and how they will.

WRITING TO ENGAGE THE BODY

Just as writing to open the body requires an awareness of the gestural and imagistic properties of language, and just as it requires an intimate awareness of the world around us, so it also requires an intimate awareness of our own bodies, an awareness of how our bodies sit and stand, walk and breathe, write and rest. I'm not saying, of course, that one needs a degree in physiology to write; rather, I am simply asking that we recognize that the body is the instrument we write with, and that we should know our instrument well. It may be tempting to argue that we write with our minds more than our bodies. But try writing with a broken finger, or a sprained wrist. At some point, our bodies must do the writing, or the writing doesn't get done. Further, what's happening to, and with, and within our bodies may well have an impact on the kind of writing we do.

In the prompts that follow, you will explore your body: its processes, its relationship to space, and its relationship to other bodies. You will also experiment with the relationship between the body and the act of writing, playing with different ways to bring your own innate physicality into your writing process. You will find, I think, that as you do so, your awareness both of writing and of your body changes. After all, writing as a spiritual practice, at the level of the body, is about suspending the stories that we think of as truth in order to reencounter the truth that arises from a focused sensual awareness. In this, we are practicing the same kind of attention required by the Buddha in his famous Lotus Sutra, wherein he simply held up a flower, and his audience became enlightened. Of course, I cannot guarantee that the prompts that follow will bring you enlightenment, but I can say that as you work through them, you will discover, in your writing and in yourself, something *illuminating*.

Sing the Body Electric

The contemporary American poet Sharon Olds, like her literary grandpa, Walt Whitman, is known widely as a writer willing to engage, discuss, describe, critique, and celebrate the human body, exploring—sometimes in clinical and/or graphic detail—the body's processes and responses. Her work, because of its unique awareness of bodily concerns, and its unwillingness to balk at "impolite" or "uncomfortable" subjects, provides an excellent opportunity to develop the bodily awareness we've been discussing. One of the remarkable things about Olds' work is the way she is able to describe the body and its functions in unflinching and frequently unflattering terms, while still celebrating their beauty and power.

Choose a bodily process to write about. Remember, you may write about *any* bodily process: giving birth, eating, sleeping, voiding the bladder and bowels, flatulence, sweating, sickness, injury, exercise, and so on. Consider writing about the beautiful and pleasurable, as well as the ugly, gross, and/or painful. Once you have selected a bodily process, describe how that process affects different parts of your body. Then write a brief description of the physical activities involved in the process. Close the exercise by finding a metaphor that speaks to the process.

Reread what you have written, and write a brief reflection on what you have written exploring how you felt about the process you selected before, during, and after writing, and why you chose the metaphor you chose.

Who's Your Deity?

Like all spiritual practices, writing lends itself to totems and rituals. A totem is an object that you have invested with power, something that you can look at or hold that helps you settle in to the task at hand—in this case, writing. In the film *Wonder Boys*, based on the novel by Michael Chabon, the writer Grady Trip writes wearing a pink ladies' dressing gown. The playwright Henrik Ibsen allegedly kept a portrait of his rival, August Strindberg, in his study. Novelist Jonathan Safran Foer keeps a framed sheet of blank paper once owned by Isaac Beshevis Singer in his living room. As for me, I like to keep a couple of gods around: Saraswati and Ganesha.

Saraswati is the Hindu goddess of wisdom, creativity, eloquence, enlightenment, music, and the arts. Her name means flowing (*saras*) wisdom (*wati*), and suggests the flow of wisdom through you onto the page or computer screen. The goddess has four arms representing mind, intellect, attention, and ego. She is often depicted playing a stringed instrument called a *vina* in two hands, with another hand holding a lotus symbolizing wisdom, and yet another holding a sacred scripture. Saraswati is called the Mother of the Vedas, the Vedas being perhaps the oldest sacred scripture of any religion.

I keep a statue of Saraswati on my desk to honor the gift of creativity that flows through me, and to remind myself that writing is a mystery that I receive and cannot control.

Sometimes, however, I am not all that open to receiving. That's where Ganesha comes in. The elephant-headed god of the Hindu pantheon, Ganesha is the Remover of Obstacles, patron of the arts and sciences, and the god of writing. According to Indian tradition, the sage Vyasa asked Ganesha to be his scribe and to write down his recitation of the *Mahābhārata*, which, along with the *Rāmāyana*, comprise the epic literature of India the way the *Iliad* and the *Odyssey* are the epic literature of the Greeks. At the heart of the *Mahābhārata* is the *Bhagavad Gītā* in which the true nature of God as source and substance of all reality is revealed in the form of Krishna.

There are many variations in Ganesha iconography. I am partial to those that show him sitting cross-legged at a writing table using a broken piece of his tusk as a pen and writing down the *Mahābhārata*. I don't worship these gods. I offer them no incense or flowers. But I do honor them every time I sit down to write. The gods are aspects of the Self, and it is the Self that I honor with my writing. So I give thanks to Saraswati for the gift of creativity, and ask Ganesha to remove the obstacles that may block my transcribing what wisdom I am privileged to hear as I sit down to write.

Of course, you may choose to keep your writing space god-free. However you choose to honor the gifts of creativity and wisdom that may come to you as you write, I urge you to do so, and not to take these gifts for granted.

As a way of reengaging with your writing space, then, and of considering the ways in which it can gift you with creativity and wisdom, I offer you the following prompt.

Settle into your writing space and look around. Describe what you see. What are the objects on your desk, or in your room? What are you sitting on? What utensils are you using to write? What talismans or totems are nearby? What distractions? Keep yourself out of these descriptions. Simply write about the objects as they appear.

Once you have your list, go back over it, and write yourself into the list. Describe the objects again in terms of what they mean to you and to your writing.

Finally, read over your second description and write a brief reflection on your space. What about the space adds to your creative flow? What detracts? How might you redesign this space to better suit your writing practice, to bring you into closer contact with the gifts of creativity and wisdom?

Our Stories, Ourselves

This exercise requires you to walk a labyrinth. Many churches have these and most are open to the public. Look online to find a labyrinth close to where you live.

A labyrinth is not a maze. Yes, I know that according to Greek legend King Minos hired Daedalus to build a labyrinth to imprison the Minotaur, but what Daedalus actually built was a maze. A maze is a complex structure with walls that forces you to make a series of directional decisions as you navigate it. Do I go right or left? The decision matters: one way leads you out of the maze, the other to a dead end or worse—one pissed-off Minotaur.

A labyrinth, on the other hand, offers you a single path without choices. Once you step onto the path it will inevitably lead you to the center, and, guess what, no Minotaur. From the center you simply retrace your steps by following the path once again, and it will lead you out to where you started.

The power of the labyrinth comes from its simplicity. Yes, it has many curves and you are led round and round in what sometimes seems an endless series of turns and returns, but if you simply surrender yourself to the path it always leads to the center and back out again. Unlike a maze, a labyrinth asks nothing more of you than to trust the path; no choice is required after the choice to trust is made.

Writing as a spiritual practice, as I never tire of reminding you, is about freeing yourself from the self. Here is one way to use the labyrinth in service to that end.

Walk the labyrinth as someone or something other than the self you think you are. If you are a twenty-something heterosexual young woman, walk the labyrinth as a fifty-something lesbian. If you are a man, walk as if you were a woman, and vice versa. Walk as a wolf, a kitten, a rock, or a leaf. There is no end to who or what you can be. Stand at the entrance to the labyrinth, speak aloud who you are walking as, recount your history (if there is one), and imagine how this self would walk (long strides, mincing steps, with determination or simple resignation). Embody this self, become who or what you just said you are. Then walk as that. When you have completed the walk, write what it was you experienced.

Sauntering

To saunter means to walk leisurely, and comes from the French *saint terre*, meaning Holy Land. It's original meaning referred to the pilgrims—some of whom were saints, most of whom were sinners and con artists—who traveled to the Holy Land beginning in the fourth century when Constantine legalized Christianity in the Roman Empire and allowed Christians to travel openly. I want to keep the notion of pilgrimage in our idea of walking, but I want to shift the Holy Land to the very ground beneath your feet.

I like walking in the city and the country; I like walking on paved sidewalks and worn forest trails. I like walking. But when walking in a city, it is more difficult to surrender to the walk. There are people to avoid hitting, and cars to avoid hitting you. So adjust yourself to your surroundings, and saunter ... meander ... wander, and for God's sake don't wear a pedometer. This isn't an aerobic race around your neighborhood, but a holy stroll into it.

Find a comfortable pace for this saunter. Walk the way Goldilocks might walk: not too slow, not too fast, just right. Carry pen (or pencil) and paper with you on your walks. I prefer 3 × 5 cards to actual sheets of paper because they are sturdy enough to write on without having to find a flat surface to lay them on. As sauntering becomes more and more part of your writing practice you will discover the muse who accompanies you on these walks is more than happy to give up her secrets. But they come swiftly and pass away quickly. The last thing you want to do is latch on to them and mull them over and over in your mind in order not to forget them. This only keeps other insights from coming to you. So jot them down, let them go, and see what comes up next.

There have been walks when I come home with pockets stuffed with cards bearing hastily scrawled notes from the muse. I admit, however, that most of these notes go nowhere. Not everything that comes to you on a walk is golden. A lot of it is just chalcopyrite: it's yellow, it's pretty, it looks like gold, but it isn't. Don't worry about it. Keep walking. The real nuggets will come.

Walking Around a Writer's Block

Writer's block is real but intangible. It is a momentary lack of anything to say that gives rise to the fear that you have nothing more to say—ever. This is just another story, and honestly, it isn't the worse thing that can happen to you. Coming to the end of speech can be a moment of blessed silence, and ought to be welcomed when it comes rather than feared. It isn't the lack of something to say or write at the moment that is the problem, but the fear generated by the story that this present quiet will extend through the rest of your life.

There are lots of ways to work with writer's block, and the one I like the most—besides blaming everyone around me for making it impossible for me to access the genius that is just below the surface of my mind—is, once again, to saunter: to walk simply for the sake of walking.

Don't walk to break the block. If you do the block becomes ever present. Just walk, saunter, meander, and let your thoughts do the same. If you can walk without purpose—walking only to walk—you will discover that your thoughts are still flowing and some of them may be worth writing down. But if not—if in fact you have come to the end of your writing career—so be it. Keep walking anyway, and look for Help Wanted signs along the way. When you've finished walking describe the act of walking: What did it feel like to "hit your stride"? What did you notice as your arms and legs moved in sync with each other? What did you see around you? Whom did you meet? How did you react? By the time you've written all this your block will be gone.

CHAPTER TWO

WRITING TO OPEN THE HEART

The second turn in our five-turn spiral is heart. In this case, of course, heart refers not to the four-chambered, blood-pumping muscle, but to the metaphorical heart—our inner reservoir of deep emotion. What I know about emotions comes from two sources: the work of Dr. Robert Plutchik (1927–2006) and the faces of my friends.

Plutchik's theory of emotion focused on what he called his "wheel of emotions," which contains eight basic emotions organized in four pairs:

Joy/Sadness
Trust/Disgust
Fear/Anger
Surprise/Anticipation

What I like about Plutchik's wheel is how simple it is. What I don't like about his wheel is that it isn't simple enough. I think the core emotions are two: love and fear. Joy, trust, and some types of surprise and anticipation are aspects of love; sadness, disgust, anger, and some types of surprise and anticipation are aspects of fear.

My reasons for focusing on this pair of love and fear are three: (1) these are easy to remember, and there is no point to having a theory that you can't remember; (2) every time I look at an emotion or experience an emotion it seems to me to be a variant of love and fear; and (3) love and fear are easy to identify: love opens the heart, fear constricts it.

When it comes to writing as a spiritual practice we want to open the heart, and to do that we have to work through fear rather than around it or avoid it altogether.

Before we go on, let me make it very clear that writing to open the heart is very different than writing "from the heart." Writing "from the heart" is a terrible cliché and, far too often, what we write when we are writing "from the heart" is terribly clichéd as well. Here's why: writing from the heart typically has nothing to do with the heart. It has to do with the head, with what we want to believe we are feeling, or what we want others to believe we are feeling. It is an act of the self rather than the Self, the narrating and narrated I rather than the unnarrated witnessing I. Writing from the heart is often the hallmark of spiritual writing, writing that is meant to soothe the self and lull the reader into spiritual smugness.

Writing to open the heart is writing as spiritual practice, writing with the intent to see what is rather than, as in the case of writing from the heart, to deny or change what is. Denying what is forces you to live a lie, and every time reality shatters a lie you are forced to scoop up the shards in an even bigger lie. Eventually, there are so many lies to manage that you can no longer identify the truth, and may even begin to doubt the very existence of truth. You become hard, cold, withdrawn, and deeply frightened. How ironic that writing from the heart, writing to deny these very emotions, can actually cause you to be controlled by them.

Writing to open the heart has nothing to do with lies because it isn't interested in denying or changing anything. Writing to open the heart is writing to see what is without measuring what is against what the self imagines should be. There is no measuring, no comparing, no transforming in writing to open the heart. There is just opening the heart to whatever it feels. Both writing from the heart and writing to open the heart engage the same fear: the fear of realizing that I am not who I think I am, that the story of me is just a story and that the I, the me of that story, is no more real (and yet no less real either) than any other character in any other work of fiction. The difference between these two types of writing is how they handle this fear. Writing from the heart seeks to deny or avoid it; writing to open the heart seeks to make room for it.

Jekyll and Hyde, or Despicable Me

All of us, at some point or another, are guilty of having done something despicable. Something that, in retrospect, or perhaps even in the midst of doing, we sensed was absolutely, without doubt, wrong. Or perhaps it wasn't "wrong," per se. Perhaps whatever it was that we did simply filled us with guilt, shame, or confusion. Typically, as we pass through these moments in life, we forgive ourselves, and forget. We make peace with the thing we have done and move on. Or perhaps we go further, making amends for our actions and working toward absolution. All of this is healthy enough; however, there is a problem. The problem is that as we absolve ourselves of our transgressions, we too often excise them from our self-story, constructing a new story that allows us to say "I am no longer the person that committed these acts." This is a form of othering. We are othering ourselves, othering the parts of us that we do not wish to acknowledge. In so doing, we create a shadow self. Never acknowledged, constantly denied.

In this prompt, we will attempt to meet our shadow self. We will do the thing that no self-help book and no psychologist on earth would recommend: we will dwell, we will relive, we will commit terrible acts (again) and feel terribly ashamed (again) ... but we will not seek forgiveness. We will, instead, seek only meeting. We will meet with the version of ourselves that lived that moment, the self that committed those crimes. We may come to an understanding with this self. We may not. But we will look it unflinchingly in the eye, reinhabiting it in order to understand it and its cruelty, cowardice, or whatever. We will meet this self without condemnation, because to condemn it is to objectify it, to buffer our current selves by imagining that this horrible thing, this enemy, is other. It isn't. We are the other. The enemy is us.

Personally, I can think of nothing I would rather not do than sit around and write about all the awful things I have done in my life. But even so, without really trying, I can think of several pretty despicable acts, several moments I am ashamed of. I would prefer not to recall them, and I would certainly prefer not to write about them, at least not publicly. If you're feeling the same way, good. Your list of crimes should make you uncomfortable. It should repel you. This is how you know it is worth investigating. I will not, of course, ask you to share your list with anyone, or to publish your writing from the list in any way. This is a private exercise, a delving into our own worst selves that need not concern anyone else. But it should concern us. Because it reminds us that the stories we tell about our worst selves are often fables; that is, fantastic tales in which we triumph over our demons the way a knight in shining armor might triumph over a terrible dragon. Of course, there is no dragon. There never was. In all our grand battles, we fought only our shadows. The goal of this exercise is to stop battling, and to recognize your shadow, to see its shape as an extension of your own.

1. Make a list of all of the despicable things you can remember doing. Don't worry about how despicable they are. Include the petty along with the vile.
2. Select the act on the list that makes you most uncomfortable at the moment and, in the first person, using concrete detail, narrate the act as an anecdote. Try to focus your narration on the immediate action, leaving out any retrospective commentary and including only those background details relevant to what happened.
3. Stop writing when you have completed your description. It need not be long, perhaps a paragraph, perhaps a page or two. Put the description away for a few days.
4. When you feel ready, return to the description you wrote and reread it. Then, take a moment to reflect on what you have read. First, focus on the character in the description as you wrote it. Ask: Who is this person? What does this act mean to him or her? Second, focus on yourself as the writer of the description. Ask: Who wrote this story? What did it mean to him or her? Finally, focus your reflection on yourself as reader. Ask: Who am I? What does this story mean to me? You may write down your reflections, or not, as you choose.

Notice that I am not asking you to do anything about the shadow side of your self. All I want you to do is observe it, and as you do you will come to see that the observer is not the observed. That is writing as spiritual practice. We'll talk about why in the next section.

ENCOUNTERING YOUR HEART

Trying to change who you are—the lowercase self, the narrated and narrating you—simply introduces never-ending conflict.

The self can never be without flaws, without its shadow, and to demand otherwise is to demand the impossible and to set the self up for failure. If you imagine that spirituality is the art of being perfect you will either never be spiritual, or the spirituality you pretend to will be a lie. Perfection in the sense of being shadow-free is impossible. What is possible is learning to observe the shadowed self from the perspective of the Self. This requires no change on the part of the self. The Self isn't asking or pretending that things are other than they are. It simply observes what is, and in that act alone it is free from being trapped by or caught up in what is.

For example, when I was a kid, my mother, in an attempt to help me get over my fear of monsters, read me a book called *There's a Monster at the End of This Book*, in which *Sesame Street's* lovable blue monster Grover tries, over and over and over again, to convince the reader not to turn to the next page because he is afraid to meet the monster waiting at the end.

His fear is real. I felt it. In fact, I delighted in it. I rejected every reason he gave for not turning a page, and deliberately turned them, one after the other. I ignored his pleading, his begging. Even when he tied pages together to prevent me from turning them, I turned them. I didn't care about his fears and feelings. His terror fed my joy. On the second-to-last page, I saw him cowering in fear, his hands covering his face.

Of course, as you've probably guessed, the monster at the end of the book is Grover himself, and everything turns out all right. It's a wonderful book, and I imagine it's supposed to be about learning to face up to fear, or about learning that some fears are irrational. Looking back on my experience, however, I see something else.

What I now see is that *I* was the monster. After all, I laughingly turned page after page even as Grover pleaded with me to stop. I had, in a way, tortured him, and I enjoyed it. The final horror at the end of the book was that I couldn't excuse what I had done. It didn't matter that Grover was OK. I hadn't known how the book was going to end, yet I'd turned the pages anyway, in complete disregard for Grover's obvious suffering. What could I have been thinking? I loved Grover! How could I do that to him?

The answer is as simple as it is stark: I am capable of terrible cruelty. I can be ruthless. And I cannot deny the streak of ruthlessness in me. In fact, I wouldn't want to. By denying it I place myself at its mercy; by insisting I cannot be cruel I am excusing any cruelty I may do as something other than cruelty.

This is part of what writing to open the heart is about: seeking, through language, an intimate encounter with the "other" within us. These encounters can and should be unsettling, but we need not fear them. Rather, we should welcome them. They offer us a chance to meet a self we never knew and to recognize that, ultimately, there is no other—there is only us. What do you do with this realization? Own it. Yes, I am capable of terrorizing a fuzzy blue monster. And, yes, I am capable of terrorizing you as well. And knowing this about myself allows me to recognize it in myself, and when I do, I can no longer allow what the heart feels to excuse what the body might do.

I'm Going to Kill You!

Have you ever been so angry that you wanted to kill someone? Did you actually do it? Maybe you did. Maybe you took this book off the library cart a guard wheeled by your cell in the maximum-security prison that is your new home. Maybe, but I doubt it. Chances are even if you felt angry enough to murder, you restrained yourself.

But murder is an extreme action; what about tearing into someone verbally? Have you ever done that? What about saying the one thing that you know hurts the other the most, and saying it in order to hurt him or her the most? Have you ever done that?

Write about those times when you allowed your feelings to excuse your behavior. Notice I said "excuse" rather than "dictate." Feelings don't make you do something, they simply excuse your doing it. The purpose of this exercise is to explore this nuance; to see that just because you feel something doesn't mean you have to act on it.

So write about a time when you were so angry that you allowed yourself to rage against another person in the most hurtful way possible. Be as detailed with your feelings and actions as possible. Try to rekindle the feelings a bit through your writing.

When you are done writing ask yourself how you feel. Then notice that the you asking how you feel isn't feeling what the you describing those feelings is feeling. The asking *you* is the Self; the feeling *you* is the self. The Self embraces the self, but isn't bound by it. The self feels this or that; the Self makes room for this and that without identifying with any of it. The self is caught by feelings; the Self is caught by nothing.

Now go back to your writing. Retell the event with this difference: at the very height of your anger introduce a new event, have a young child enter the scene frightened, screaming, maybe even covered in blood. She desperately needs your help. What do you do? Yes, this is fiction, go with it. What do you do? What are you feeling as you realize this child is in terrible trouble? Write this all down. And then ask yourself what happened to the anger you felt a moment before the child entered the scene? Where did it go? If you were that anger, are you someone else when it is gone? Are you only the creation of your feelings? Or are you something else, something greater than this feeling or that feeling, this self and that self?

You can't write about this something greater, for as soon as you do it is something else, something less. But you can use writing to sense the Self behind the writing, and that is good enough.

Automatic Writing

The heart is a broad country, and not all of its provinces are ruled by the wicked. Some are joyous, some loving; some are cold and calculating; some are arrogant; some ambitious. Some lie entirely outside our knowledge. This prompt is a gateway to all of them.

Automatic writing is a type of writing that allows us to evade the conscious mind and plumb the subconscious. Once upon a time, spiritualists imagined that automatic writing amounted to a kind of otherworldly contact, a channeling of supernatural forces from the great beyond. Psychiatrists today argue that automatic writing is the result of the ideomotor effect, essentially a kind of reflex of the temporal lobes and limbic system, which together govern emotion, instinct, and inspiration as well as the drive to communicate. Of course, usually, the ideas and words that originate in the temporal lobes are further edited and organized by the frontal lobe. But through automatic writing, we can do an end run around this internal editor, and get access to the raw script, or first draft, of our ongoing interior monologue.

For this reason, automatic writing became an important part of the surrealist movement in twentieth-century Western literature and culture. The surrealists were interested in exploring what their founder, the French poet André Breton, called "pure psychic automatism," a broad term comprising any process by which a person seeks to express the pure functioning of thought without the control exercised by reason, aesthetics, or morality.

It was the surrealists who developed, as an artistic parlor game, a system for triggering automatic writing. Our prompt is based on the rules of their game:

1. Sit at your desk with a pen and paper (or with your computer, tablet, netbook) and put yourself in a "receptive" frame of mind.
2. Begin writing. Write whatever comes to mind, and write as quickly as possible, without pausing.
3. If for some reason the flow stops, leave a space and immediately begin writing again on a new line beginning with a randomly chosen letter of the alphabet. Choose the letter before you begin, and always begin new lines with the same letter.
4. Write this way for as long as you can. It may help to set a timer, and to gradually increase the length of your sessions.

This is the basic game, but there is a variation you may try if you wish to further investigate some of the ideas or images that arise from these automatic sessions. Once you have at least one automatic writing session under your belt, read back over your writing and select a single sentence, phrase, or image that resonates with you. Then begin a new automatic writing session with that sentence, phrase, or image. You can actually do this recursively, writing for a set period of time, then rereading and starting over with a new sentence, phrase, or image drawn from the most recent piece of writing.

The writing you do during these sessions may or may not make sense—in fact, it most likely will not. Nevertheless, in this writing you may discover thoughts and feelings you never knew you had, or vivid images (or image patterns) that surface unexpectedly with the potency of dreams. Hold fast to these. Uncomfortable or baffling or silly as they may appear, they are missives from the unmapped regions of your heart. In them, you may see yourself illuminated.

ENCOUNTERING THE HEARTS OF OTHERS

So far we have been talking about encountering aspects of your self; now let's talk about encountering others. In this context, opening the heart means being present to others in a way that makes you vulnerable to hurt, grief, and suffering. Indeed, it is in your capacity to hurt, grieve, and suffer that you discover your capacity to love. If you can't be hurt, you can't love because you are too defended to let another in. If you can't grieve, you can't love because you have restricted your feelings for another to such a low level that allows for no deep sense of loss if the other leaves or dies. If you can't suffer, you can't have compassion with others who do suffer. Compassion comes from the Latin *com* (shared) *passion* (suffering). Compassion is the capacity to suffer together, and this requires an open heart rather than a constricted one.

Yet here is where most of us fall down. We have compassion, for our friends and family, for our neighbors, for those caught up in calamity—hurricanes, tornadoes, earthquakes, famine, disease—but sometimes, too often, our compassion serves our convenience. Sometimes we cannot muster compassion at all. This is why I am more moved by Jesus' admonishment to "love your enemy" (Matthew 5:44) than I am by his (and Leviticus') command to "love your neighbor" (Leviticus 19:18; Mark 12:31). Loving my neighbor is relatively easy. I mean, yes, her dogs scamper about the yard at odd hours, and when her nephew and niece are around the scampering becomes bounding and barking, screaming and crashing, and that is ... well, annoying. But in the end, it's minor, and it doesn't really get in the way of our having a perfectly pleasant, neighborly relationship.

Loving my enemies, on the other hand, is a hell of a thing. I *fear* my enemies. And with good reason: they're out to get me. That's why we're enemies. To imagine loving them makes me nervous to say the least. What does it mean, anyway? Am I supposed to make peace with them? What if they don't want peace? Or what if the terms of peace are unacceptable? How am I supposed to forgive all the awful things they did to me, and how are they supposed to forgive all the awful things I did to them? The answer is: I'm not. They're not. Jesus doesn't say forgive your enemies. He doesn't say make peace with them. He doesn't even say not to *have* enemies. He tells us, instead, to love them.

So the real question isn't "what does it mean to love my enemy?" but "what does it mean to love at all?" What does it mean to love somebody?

Jefferson Airplane, the '60s rock group, gives us a hint. In the song "Somebody to Love," lead singer Grace Slick sings, "When the truth is found to be lies, and all the joy within you dies, don't you want somebody to love?"

Is this true? The song was written by Darby Slick, Grace's brother-in-law, and originally recorded by his folk-rock band, the Great Society. The Airplane came out with their psychedelic version a few years later. The song is listed among *Rolling Stone*'s "500 Best Rock Songs," and is featured in many movies, most recently *A Serious Man*, the Coen brothers' retelling of the Book of Job. No doubt it is popular, but is it true?

When the truth is found to be lies, and everything within you dies, is love the answer? Is love the antidote to despair? Yes and no. No, love isn't the antidote to despair, but, yes, love may be what emerges when you discover that all you thought was true was a lie.

I was once driving too fast through a school zone. I hadn't seen the sign, and was paying no attention to the fact that elementary school kids were being picked up. I sped along the street according to the nonschool-zone speed limit. A guy driving behind me in a white Ford F-150 pickup truck honked and waved at me to slow down. I noticed him, realized what I was doing, and quickly cut my speed for the few yards of school zone left to me. I rolled down my window and waved at the man in gratitude and shouted, "Thank you!" I really had been oblivious. I swear I waved with all five fingers, but he saw only one. And my "thank you" must have been drowned out in the noise of the school kids, and all he heard was the "k" and the "you." As soon as he was clear of the school zone he revved his engine and the big Ford was after me. I panicked, and picked up speed. He did the same.

At the time I owned a Porsche 944S. It is important to make note of the S (sport) because it made this Porsche more than an entry-level Porsche. If you are going to drive a Porsche, and a red one at that, you don't want people to think you could only afford an entry-level model. Truth is, I didn't buy the car new; in fact, I didn't buy it at all. I ghost wrote a book for a friend who was selling the car, and took it in exchange. The point of all this is to say that a Porsche 944S can outrun a Ford F-150 on any open road. The problem was that we weren't on an open road, and this guy was on my tail no matter what I did.

Finally, I decided to confront him. I slipped into the left-hand lane of a two-lane street, rolled down the passenger-side window as I pulled up to a red light, and waited for the Ford pickup to pull alongside. I kept my hands on the steering wheel where he could see them so he knew I was unarmed, and hoped to God he wasn't packing heat and itching for a gun fight.

The driver of the Ford leaned out of his window menacingly. The blood was rushing through his face and he was boiling mad. I smiled, lifted my hand in a wave again and said, "I said, 'Thank you.'" This time he heard me. His face was still red, not with anger this time but with embarrassment. His body softened and he quickly told me that his daughter had been hit by a car racing through that very school speed zone a few months ago. She was OK, but he was a passionate defender of school zone safety.

I think I saw tears in his eyes as he told me about his little girl, and I felt a shock of horror at the thought that I could have hit someone as well. When the light changed, he sat back, waved, and drove off. I let him get ahead of me. I was driving a Porsche 944S—don't forget the S—and had nothing to prove.

What does this have to do with loving your enemies? I don't want to make too much of it, but, as he was telling me about his daughter, I was listening with every fiber of my being, and we made a connection. There was love there. Not romantic love; not the love that keeps Viagra in business, but another kind of love: the love that happens when people—even frightened, angry people—let go of their fears and share their truths.

Back to Grace Slick. The fellow in the Ford had his truth: I was a narcissistic maniac who put kids in danger and gave the finger and a hearty *f you* to anyone who tried to stop me. When he found this truth to be a lie (sure I'm narcissistic, but the rest of it isn't true) the result was a genuine meeting. He found somebody to love. Me. For a moment.

When Jesus says, to "love your enemies," I think he is challenging us to meet them, to get to know them for who they are rather than who we imagine them to be. Genuine meeting leads to love. This is why Psalm 23 tells us that God prepares a banquet for you in the presence of your enemies (Psalm 23:5). God isn't doing this to taunt your enemies. You aren't expected to sit down to eat in front of them in a hubristic act of "nah, nah, nah-nah nah." The table is set in front of your enemies so that you can invite them to sit with you and eat, and when they do, and when you start to share your truths, perhaps you will no longer be enemies.

Dining with the Devil

Make a list of your enemies. If you can't come up with any real enemies, make a list of people whom you strongly dislike. Now invite them to dinner. Not literally, but literarily.

Write about having dinner with these people. Prepare and serve a meal that pleases both you and them. Write about how you would welcome them; how you would explain the invitation and the purpose of the meal. Make it clear that you invited them to hear their truths and share your own. And write about their truths. Yes, this is an act of fictional writing. You may not know their truths, but do your best to extrapolate their truths from the behaviors you actually see them exhibit in real life. Notice what happens to your body and your heart as you write about their truths. Can you sense your body softening and your heart opening? Do this exercise over and over until you do.

Dear Hated One

The hardest person to love is someone you define as an enemy. To love the enemy, of course, you have to meet him. This is not always a good idea. Enemies tend to meet over pistols at dawn, and it's very tricky to remain radically open when your safety demands you run for cover or strap on a bulletproof vest. So, rather than trying to track down your enemy for a face-to-face, I suggest meeting him or her in another way: in a love letter.

Two things before you get started on this exercise. First, let's be very clear: do not mail these letters. This is not a book about how to mend relationships. This is a book about how to use writing to turn the spiral of body, heart, mind, soul, and spirit. This is an exercise for opening the heart, not baring it to someone else. So, again, do not mail these letters. In fact, if you are writing them on your computer, delete them when you are done. If you are using actual paper, burn them. Or shred them. And if you shred them, then burn them. Just DO NOT MAIL THEM.

I say this because I know people who have mailed them. These people were shredded. And burned. So, please, no mailing.

Second, the goal of this exercise is to awaken your heart to a very specific idea: people, even the people you hate, are doing the best they can with what they've got. This may be a difficult idea for you to swallow. Most of us like to think that people have absolute free will, that they can act however they choose, and that when they act like jerks it is because they choose to act like jerks. I would like to suggest an alternative view.

Free will is a very limited factor in your life. While in theory you do have a variety of options at any given moment regarding actions you may take, the truth is your past has conditioned you so powerfully that most of your options are simply unchoosable. You do what you do because you have done it so often. To put it as simply as I can: most of the time you act on autopilot.

What is true of you is true of everyone. While there are exceptions, and these can be major, most people who hurt you never set out to hurt you. They are just doing what they imagine they have to do in order to get what they imagine they have to get, and you are merely collateral damage.

Think of the last time a close friend did something that hurt you. Perhaps she kept a secret from you, or perhaps you said something and she exploded with such venom that for a moment you had no idea with whom you were talking; your friend was gone, replaced by an alien who had invaded her body. Did she set out to harm you by keeping that secret? Or was she simply protecting herself? Was she looking for an opening to unleash her wrath, or was she as surprised as you at the level of her anger?

Only you can say, but only she can know. The aim of this exercise to imagine what she knows. This is how it works:

Sit down at your computer or with paper and pen, and write your friend a letter. Explain the situation as you felt it. Explain how hurt you were, and maybe still are. This event doesn't have to be a recent one. We aren't trying to rekindle old emotions, but to recognize a timeless truth: most often people do what they do because at the moment they do it, doing it is all they can do.

After you have set out your side of the story, shift your imagination to her side. As best you can, write about the situation from her perspective. Don't pretend to be her and write an excuse for her behavior. Write an analysis suggesting why her behavior was, given the situation at that moment, inevitable. This may be difficult—it is meant to be; we are too ready to ascribe premeditation to situations where there is none in order to blame the other for our hurt feelings, and this exercise is going to reveal a different perspective.

Once you have completed your analysis of the other's behavior, take a second look at your own. Why did you feel hurt or angry or betrayed? Could you have felt any other way at that moment, or were you as conditioned as your friend? I think you will find that the latter is true.

I'm not saying people are robots; I'm saying that we humans are conditioned by our past to act in certain ways in the present, and only a huge effort of will can free us from that conditioning. It can be done, but few of us are willing to do it. It isn't that we are selfish or uncaring, but that we have lots of other things to do with our time, and, really, what we did wasn't so bad after all, and we never meant to hurt anybody, and if you are hurt it really isn't our fault, and you should get over it so we can get on with it. You get the idea.

What does this exercise do for you? It helps you realize that we are all trapped in our past, conditioned by our past, and victims of habit. This realization need not excuse an action, nor is it necessarily the basis for forgiveness. We are doing this to soften the heart. We are doing this to realize that our hardened hearts are hardened automatically by forces beyond our conscious control. We are doing this because as we do it we discover compassion arising: compassion for the other and compassion for ourselves. We realize that we are all doing the best we can with what we've got to work with at the moment, and often what we've got isn't all that wonderful or helpful. But it is what we've got, and who we are, and who the other person is, and we are all trapped and suffering in those traps, and really we need to cry together over our stuckness rather than rage at each other under the banner of an imagined freedom.

This would be the opportune time to share a sample letter with you, but I have shredded all of mine, and burned the shredded strips, so all I could do here is make up something, and rather than read something I make up, you would be better off writing your own. What I can do is share some comments e-mailed to me from people who have done this exercise.

I thought this was going to be a complete waste of time, and, to be honest, it started out that way. Then, about halfway through writing the story from the other person's perspective I realized something: he was a victim. I started recalling things he had told me about his growing up with an alcoholic father and suicidal mother who did eventually kill herself. I remembered how he often had thoughts of suicide. And then, all of a sudden, I saw what he had said to me as a script he was compelled to read aloud. I don't think he wrote it, he simply adapted it to me. I now suspect he has read this script many times with many people and that is why he is so alone and so often lonely.

I started to feel sorry for him, and I thought that was the point of the exercise. Then I went back to my own telling of the event and saw that I was just as trapped in my own script. I stopped feeling sorry for him. Feeling sorry gave me the moral high ground, but there was no moral high ground. There were just two people trapped in their pasts trying to maintain the illusion that they were free in the present. I felt sorry for both of us. And then I think that feeling turned into compassion and that, at least a little, into love.

I really wanted to send this Dear Hated One to the person to whom I wrote it. I didn't, but I wanted to. And the reason I wanted to was that I think it revealed just how messed up we both are, and how that's OK—it's just the way it is—and that recognizing that frees us from having to blame one another for what happened. On the contrary, it allows us to empathize with each other for being so compelled to do what we do when we really want to do something else. Being trapped is comforting as long as you don't know your trapped. Being trapped and knowing you're trapped is frustrating. But what's worse, being trapped and knowing you're trapped and knowing that once you know it you can work to be free of that trap is actually terrifying. Can I be so trapped that I would rather be trapped than free?

The answer to that last question is yes. You can be just that trapped. But there is hope. The hope isn't that you can break the shackles that bind you, but that knowing you are trapped no longer allows you to pretend you are free. Once you stop mistaking imprisonment for freedom, you only have two choices: live the story of your entrapment or live a different story.

It is all about story. You are only the stories you tell. Tell stories of entrapment and you are entrapped. Tell stories of liberation and you can be free. Of course, the telling can't come from the same self that is entrapped. A constricted heart choked by the mind's story of justified hate and mistaken freedom cannot free itself. What it can do, what this exercise is designed to do, is make it clear to the mind that it is the problem. Once this is clear to the mind, there is a chance of opening to the soul, and the soul is never anything but free.

GENUINE MEETING: ENCOUNTERING THE HEART OF ALL

Martin Buber, the twentieth-century Jewish philosopher famous for his philosophy of dialogue, puts meeting at the heart of his teaching. "All real living," Buber writes in his brilliant classic *I and Thou*, "is meeting." By "meeting" (*Begegnung*), Buber means what happens when two people step out of their private spheres and fully engage one another in the moment, holding nothing back. This can happen between people, between people and animals, between people and nature, between people and art or music, and between people and

God. The key is that the "other" is seen as a *thou*, a whole being, and not as a means to some end you have in mind. I believe that is what happened between that father and me. Our meeting at the stoplight met Buber's requirement that the encounter be immediate, personal, and reciprocal. For Buber, such meetings cannot be planned, and there is no training one can undergo to have them. It is a reality that unfolds of its own accord whenever you encounter another being as *thou*. I believe you are ripe for such a meeting when you are shattered: when all of the love within you dies; when reality puts you in a situation where you have no choice but to be fully, personally, present to another. This is finding someone to love.

The kind of finding we are talking about has nothing to do with Christiansingles.com, or Jdate, or eHarmony.com. This is not an active seeking out, but an emptying of self that allows any encounter to become genuine meeting.

Most encounters fail to become genuine meetings. Sticking with Ms. Slick for a moment, Grace and I sat together before a Jefferson Airplane concert in Springfield, Massachuetts. This must have been in 1968. I was features editor of the Longmeadow High School newspaper and had managed to get two press passes to the concert that got backstage access to the band for my friend and editor in chief, Bob Bessel, and me. We were alone with the band as they prepared for the show.

Bob sat on the floor with Jorma Kaukonen, the band's guitarist, and I sat next to Grace on a table top. Bob had a million questions to ask; I couldn't think of one. Grace simply ignored me; after all, I wasn't saying anything. Unfortunately, I couldn't ignore me as well: "For God's sake, man, you are sitting next to Grace Slick—say something!"

Saying something isn't the same as saying anything, but at the time anything was all that came to mind. A copy of *Vogue* magazine was lying on the table. I picked it up and said to Grace, "Is this yours?"

That's it. That's all I had. As it turned out, it wasn't hers, and we had nothing more to talk about for the next few minutes, which in "I am the biggest jackass on the planet" time felt like years. There was an encounter, but there was no meeting. The problem was I was trying too hard. My friend Bob just plopped himself down on the floor next to Jorma and started talking, assuming something of value would come out. I sat next to Grace and tried to script the perfect conversation:

> I would say, "Given that you were born in 1939 and hence lived as a young girl during World War II, how do you think your experiences during the war influenced your experiences with psychedelics some three decades later?"
>
> And she would say, "An excellent question, and one I have often pondered, but one that rarely comes up in the more superficial interviews I have had with magazines like *Ramparts* and *Rolling Stone*. Have you won a Pulitzer with your work on your school paper?"

OK, maybe a bit over the top, but still a helluva lot better than, "Is this your magazine?" I will never forgive myself for this. Never.

Anyway, my point is that true meeting requires trust: trust in yourself, trust in the other, and trust in the moment to ripen as it will. It also requires fearlessness: the fearlessness to be vulnerable, to open yourself to the risks of encounter without regard for the ego and its script. This, then, is what it means to love: to meet the other with radical openness, with fearless trust, compassion, and vulnerability. This goes for loving enemies, neighbors, friends, family, total strangers, and yourself. And, should the opportunity arise, it also goes for loving Grace Slick.

Cultivating this kind of love is the most fundamental goal of writing to open the heart. It is key not only to meeting the other within yourself, not only to meeting other people, but to meeting

God as well. Meeting God is a terrifying thing, more terrifying than encountering your own inner demons, your enemies, or the coolest of rock stars. It is terrifying not because we fear God's judgment—this is simply a dodge—but because in that meeting with the divine the self is annihilated. Jews call this moment of self-annihilation *bittul hayesh*; Christians call it "dying to self"; for Sufis it is *fana*; and Buddhists call it nirvana. Regardless of the tradition, the idea is that, in the encounter with the unnamed and unnameable heart of reality, we cannot sustain our own identity: the ego's story dissolves, and the self becomes at once no one/ nothing, and everyone/everything.

The Bible is, of course, full of stories of meeting God. In each, there comes a moment of startling pain and heartrending incomprehension in which the self that was dissolves and a new self emerges. For Abram, it is the moment when he is called to leave his country, his kin, and his parents for an undisclosed destination (Genesis 12:1). For Jacob, it is the wrestling match with the angel, after which he receives a new name: Israel (Genesis 32:23–34). For Moses, it is the meeting with God at the burning bush, during which he is commanded to leave his comfortable life as a shepherd and return to Egypt to free the Hebrew slaves (Exodus 3:1–21). For Jonah, it is the moment in which he is tossed into the sea to calm the anger of God (Jonah 1:11–15). For Job, it is the encounter with the whirlwind—a metaphor for the inexplicable nature of the divine (Job 38:1).

In each story, the hero comes face-to-face with the ineffable nature of the universe and is transformed. But not without loss, not without grief and suffering. For some, the pain is physical; for others, emotional or psychological. But the bottom line is that in encountering the divine we must be prepared to lose everything we think we are.

Meeting God, then, represents perhaps the greatest threat to the egoic I, to the lowercase self. So we are, quite naturally, afraid. But if we can make room for our fear, which is the ego's fear of dissolution, and embrace with love the death of self, then we may find ourselves again on the other side of the encounter, trembling in the midst of life. This is the widest opening of the heart. We began by meeting the other in ourselves, and then in our neighbors and enemies, and now finally in the divine. Each encounter allows us to step beyond the boundaries of our small self and the stories it tells to maintain itself, and when we do we are irrevocably changed. We discover that we are not who we believed we were, and that the "other" is and has always been part of ourselves. Then we forget.

We grow comfortable in our new identities, new selves, new stories, until a genuine meeting happens again, and we are again transformed. The prompts that follow are designed to help you move toward such meetings. The order of the prompts follows the spiraling outward of the heart, moving from encounters with our own hearts to encounters with the hearts of those around us, and finally to encounters with the ineffable heart of reality.

Heart Lines 1

Heart Lines is an exercise that uses short verses from both the Bible's book of Psalms and the Sufi poet Rumi to give you a jumping-off point for writing from the heart. You can, of course, use other sources as well.

The book of Psalms in the Hebrew Bible is a rich source of heart writing. In Hebrew, the book is called *Sefer Tehillim*, Book of Praises. The English *psalm* comes from the Greek *psalmoi*, which may have referred to poems sung to the sound of a lyre or harp. The book of Psalms contains 150 songs of praise, though the Septuagint, the second-century BCE Greek translation of the Hebrew Bible, includes a 151st psalm that is not considered canonical by all Bible users.

The Jewish and Christian traditions hold that David, who became king of Israel, was the author of all 150 psalms, though he may have modeled his poems on older songs composed by Moses and other prophets. In Islam, the book of Psalms is called *Zabur* and is mentioned in the Qur'an. Muslims believe that the Psalms were revealed to David the way Torah was revealed to Moses and the Qur'an to Muhammad.

The scholarly opinion on the origins of the book of Psalms is open to debate, with some scholars arguing that they were written prior to the sixth century BCE and others after it. If you like to argue these kinds of things, be my guest, but my interest in Psalms is neither historical nor theological. Whatever their value to Jewish and Christian liturgy (and they are central to both), I am interested in using Psalms—or more accurately, specific passages taken from the Psalms—as prompts for further heart work. I call this practice Psalm Lines.

Remember, our goal here is not to write beautiful poetry, but to use writing as a process of turning the spiral from body to heart to mind to soul to spirit and back again. Turning the heart aspect of the spiral is about opening the heart to its primal emotions—love and fear—and then moving into and through these in ways that allow us to embrace both while being caught up in neither. This is not to say we don't feel anything, or to imply that love is the same as fear and neither should touch us. Rather, I am saying that we should experience love and fear without desire or aversion. When there is love—love! When there is fear—fear! No judgment, just wholehearted presence to whatever we are feeling.

This is the deeper work of turning the heart portion of the spiral. We are freeing ourselves to feel whatever arises by freeing ourselves from the need to physically respond to whatever is felt. We can feel the fear and not flee or lash out in anger; we can feel the love and not embrace or imagine it to be something it isn't. We are free to feel whatever we feel because we are free from the compulsion to act on our feelings.

One way to engage in this self-observation is to use a line from the Psalms as a prompt to your own writing. For example:

Begin with this: "Judge me, Searcher of Hearts, according to my integrity" (Psalm 7:9–10). Take this line as a catalyst to your own words. Write quickly; don't think, just feel. What comes after "Judge me, Searcher of Hearts, according to my integrity"? Here is an example of my own:

Judge me, Searcher of Hearts, according to my integrity; my integrity
not my hungers or my fears. My integrity
not my fleeting thoughts or pounding feelings.
My integrity: my promise, not my fame;
My potentiality not my actuality.
Set the bar high
and trip me up
whenever I seek to walk under it.

What does this mean? I have no idea, and in any case it is beside the point. Don't analyze or edit your writing, just write. Analyzing and editing bring in the powers of mind, and the need to write well and maybe publish and become famous. We will deal with mind later. For now, we are simply writing to open the heart: letting whatever is in us at the moment pour out of us onto the page.

What follows are some lines from the book of Psalms. They are not literal translations of the Hebrew. In preparing these prompts I wrote what I heard when reading the Hebrew, or looking at various English translations. Don't worry about their literary accuracy. They are prompts, not bits of revelation. If you prefer to use texts drawn from the Bible yourself, please do that. Open the text at random and scan the page until a line or phrase speaks to you, and then speak to it. What I offer here are some examples to get you started.

1. The One Who Is said to me, "You are my child! This day I birth you!" (Psalm 2:7)
2. I lie down. I sleep. I awake. It is You who sustains me! (Psalm 3:6)
3. Judge me, Searcher of Hearts, by my integrity. (Psalm 7:9–10)
4. What are we humans that You remember us; we who die, that You are mindful of us? Yet You made us little lower than God! (Psalm 8:4–5)
5. Help me, Beloved, for simplicity is lost, and all honesty has vanished from my heart. (Psalm 12:2)
6. You bring me to spaciousness. You free me because You desire me. (Psalm 18:20)
7. My God! My God! Why have You abandoned me? (Psalm 22:9)
8. Beloved, make me sovereign over my passions ... gladden me with the joy of Your company. (Psalm 21:2, 7)
9. Beloved, with You as my shepherd, what more could I want? (Psalm 23:1)
10. Beloved, train me in Your truth, and teach me. For You are salvation; I ache for You always. (Psalm 25:4–5)
11. Through the deafening pounding of my heart You whisper: "Seek my face!" (Psalm 27:8)
12. Beloved, I cannot hide my sighing. (Psalm 38:22)

13. The taunts of my enemies I can bear; the raised fist of a foe I can detect; but the treachery of a friend—this will slay me. (Psalm 54:13–14)
14. Beloved, You do not hunger for sacrifice, but desire only the contrite and broken heart. (Psalm 51:18–19)
15. Lift me, my Beloved, to a rock beyond the storm. There I will dwell and find refuge in Your sheltering Presence. (Psalm 61:4–5)

Heart Lines 2: Rumi-nations

The thirteenth-century Persian Sufi poet Jalal al-Din Muhammad Rumi was one of the greatest mystics and theologians of all time. While steeped in the history, wisdom, and practices of Islam, Rumi lifted his faith to heights that allowed him to speak to all humanity of a single truth: the presence of God in every beating heart.

Born in Balkh, Afghanistan, on September 30, 1207 (he died on December 17, 1273), Rumi moved with his family at the insistence of his father, Baha' ud-Din Waled, who either feared the machinations of the ruling families or the threat of Mongol invasion, or both, and spent most of his life in Konya, in what is today Turkey.

Rumi's two great teachers were his father, a well-respected and powerful Sufi sheikh with many followers, and Shams-i Tabriz, a wandering Sufi saint who prayed to Allah to help him find someone who could endure the spiritual wildness of his company. According to legend, Shams heard a voice, presumably that of an angel sent by Allah, who asked him, "What will you give (for the privilege of such a companion)?" Shams answered unhesitatingly, "My head!" "The one you seek," the voice continued, "is Jalal al-Din of Konya." The two men met on November 15, 1244, and Rumi's life was changed forever.

It is not the purpose of this book to explicate the life of Rumi and his transformative friendship with Shams-i Tabriz, but their love for one other is as deep and passionate as that of David and Jonathan in the Bible and far better chronicled. When Shams mysteriously disappeared on December 5, 1248—most likely murdered by students of Rumi jealous of the influence of Shams over their master—Rumi found an outlet for his grief by writing a series of poems collected under the title *Divan-i Shams-i Tabriz.*

Rumi had been spontaneously composing and reciting *ghazals* (Persian poems) for a long time, and these are collected in a volume called *Divan-i Kabir*, but it was a suggestion by his student Hussam al-Din Chalabi that led him to his masterpiece.

The two men had been walking in the vineyards outside Konya when Hussam suggested that Rumi write a book of poems that wandering troubadours could put to music and spread wherever they traveled. Rumi then reached into his pocket, pulled out a piece of paper, and read to Hussam the first eighteen verses of what he hoped would be just such a book. With the support of Hussam, Rumi moved to Kohya, where he dictated to Hussam his six-volume masterpiece, the *Mathnawi.*

Rumi was a poet of the heart, opening the heart by speaking to the heart's longing for companionship both human and divine. In this prompt I use lines from Rumi's poems the same way I used lines from the book of Psalms: as springboards to discovering your own heart song. Do not dwell on the verses provided or on others I hope you will discover as you read Rumi for yourself. I have deliberately avoided citing "chapter and verse" with these quotes. I'm not encouraging you to look up the longer poems from which they come. Indeed, these are my own free rendering of the Persian and not scholarly translations. Pick a verse (or find one on your own), copy it out on a sheet of paper or on your computer, and let flow from your heart what is triggered by Rumi's words.

My every breath says, "Humble me! Humble me!
When I am reduced to naught God's glory will be
known."

My grief imprisons me. Look! The key is here!

Death will take from me all that I have. Quick! Let
me give it all away that Death find me empty.

Don't go out in search of the moon. The Moon you
seek is inside you.

Beseech God: "Beloved, illuminate me!" And
beware, for your torch may set the world on fire.

Polish your heart diligently, and in time you will see
both the good and the bad.

Collapse in God's arms and you'll weep like a child.
Refuse Him and you will become cold as ice.

God is an ocean of mercy; come and cleanse your
faults.

I am shrouded of shadows; blind me with Light!

If it is love you seek, decapitate fear.

Don't despair if God sends you away. Tomorrow
you may be called back.

CHAPTER THREE

WRITING TO OPEN THE MIND

Mind is the third turning of the spiral. It is the most fertile aspect of the spiral for spiritual development because it is the part of us that is the most confused. The body, for example, knows what it is supposed to do, and for the most part knows how to do it.

There is a tradition in Judaism of reciting a prayer of thanks after going to the bathroom. The prayer is called *Asher yatzar*, meaning "One who has formed humanity." After using the toilet you are to wash your hands and recite the prayer:

> Blessed are You, Ineffable God, Source and Substance of all reality, Who formed me with wisdom, and created within me many openings and closings. If that which should open remain closed, or that which should close open incorrectly, it would be impossible for me to survive and stand before You. Blessed are You, Ineffable One, Who heals all flesh with wondrous acts beyond my control.

Think about this for a moment. You do not control your bodily functions. Sure, you can eat right, exercise, and drink enough Metamucil to drown an elephant, but if the body isn't working, it isn't working, and there isn't much you can do about it. Thankfully, most of us have bodies that work pretty well most of the time. Of course, in time, this will not be the case, but the point is that, whether it's working well or working poorly, the body does what it does beyond your conscious control.

Test this out for yourself. Take a deep breath, and hold it for about thirty minutes.... Chances are you barely made it to three minutes, let alone thirty. Or try this: stop your heart from beating, or your toenails from lengthening, or your nose hairs from growing.

You can't do it.

You can't do it because most of the essential work your body does happens way below the level of consciousness. Indeed, the conscious mind has no access whatsoever to the mechanisms the body uses to maintain itself. You simply have to trust the body to do what it needs to do as best it can.

What is true of the body is true of the heart as well: you rarely if ever choose your feelings. You simply feel one way or another, notice that you are feeling one way or another, and then look for a reason to explain or excuse why you are feeling one way or another. The feelings just happen; the explanation is your conscious act.

Most of us don't like to think this way. We like to imagine that we are in control of our feelings, but if this were true, you wouldn't ever feel sad, depressed, angry, bitter, or hateful. If you could choose, you would choose to feel happy, joyous, and fulfilled. But you have no choice. Feelings arise of their own accord; the only choice you have is what to do with them.

So the heart does what it does, feels what it feels, and you only notice what you are feeling after the heart is already feeling it. If this idea upsets you, ask yourself this: Did you choose to get upset about this idea or did upset feelings just happen, and you are now noticing them? And if you did choose to get upset, why did you make that choice? Who would choose to be upset when you could choose to be happy and just put this book aside? All I am saying is: the body and heart know what they are doing; the mind, however, is a different story. Literally. When we are talking about the mind we are talking about the self, the egoic I, that self-conscious part of you that identifies as you. The body and heart are conscious, but not self-conscious. The body doesn't compare itself to others, worrying that it is too fat, too thin, too hairy, too flat-chested, too bosomy. The heart doesn't say, "I should feel this way, and it is wrong to feel that way." But the mind does. In fact, making self-judgments and comparing oneself to others is one of the main preoccupations of the mind. The self maintains its sense of self by insisting on being "other than" other selves.

This is true both of individuals and of communities. The idea that the individual imagines the other as a way of defining the borders of the self is an old one, and many philosophers— from Hegel to Husserl to Sartre to Simone de Beauvoir—have made use of it. In terms of community, we may say much the same thing. Racial, ethnic, religious, and political communities each establish a circumscribed set of identifiers (skin color, eye shape, a set of beliefs and behaviors, a specific historical narrative or geographic location, and so forth) that allow them to establish and maintain definite borders. This is natural, and necessary, but not *real*. Maps change, countries rise and fall, paradigms shift, and even racial and ethnic identity are not set in stone.

For example, in 1866, after the Civil War and the abolition of slavery, the Cherokee Nation signed a treaty with the U.S. government guaranteeing tribal citizenship for African Americans who had worked on Cherokee-owned plantations in the South. But recently, the Cherokee Nation decided it would no longer honor this treaty, and the tribal leadership ousted 2,800 African American freedmen, the descendants of freed Cherokee slaves, who, up until now, had been considered Cherokee. Of course, the ousted Cherokee still identify as Cherokee, and the U.S. government (refusing the decision of the Cherokee leadership) still identifies them as Cherokee. There are two points here. First, what constitutes identity is clearly ambiguous and flexible: a matter of legality, social convention, politics, and personal allegiance, rather than a matter of some intrinsic objective truth. Second, the way in which we determine our identity has significant real-world ramifications. The people we claim as our own (those we identify as "us") are granted a voice and a place in our communities, while those we decide are "other" (those we identify as "them or "not us") are marginalized—the Cherokee freedmen, to continue our example, have been barred from voting in tribal elections and can no longer receive benefits from the Cherokee Nation.

All this points to the power of story, and the mind's ability to spin stories of consequence. In the Cherokee leadership's story, Cherokee identity is a matter of genetics, traced through blood relations. But in the freedmen's story, it is a matter of over a century's worth of shared tradition and community. Two stories, competing for the status of "truth."

And this is where we begin to run into serious problems. The competition for "truth-value" is not academic. It is passionate and, far too often, bloody. What is more, it often involves the emergence of a nasty strain of fundamentalist storytelling: stories that are self-limiting; stories that demean the body and constrict the heart; stories that alienate the self and demonize the other; stories that validate hatred, oppression, and murder.

Here is a prime example of such a story from the Hebrew Bible:

> When you approach a city to do battle, first, offer its inhabitants terms of peace. If they accept and open the city to you, you shall enslave the populace and they shall serve you. But if they refuse your terms and make war, besiege

the city until the Lord your God gives it to you. Then you shall take your swords and put to death all its males, but the women, the children, the cattle and all the city's wealth you shall take for yourselves as spoils of war. Enjoy your plunder for the Lord your God has given it to you.

This is how you shall treat all the cities outside the land, but as regards the cities in the land that the Lord your God gives you for an inheritance, you shall act differently. In these cities you shall slaughter all life: everything that breathes. This is the command of the Lord your God: Completely destroy the Hittites and the Amorites, the Canaanites and the Perizzites, the Hivites and the Jebusites that they not live to teach you to serve their gods, and in this way cause you to sin against the Lord your God. (Deuteronomy 20:10–18; my translation)

This is a chicken-and-egg issue. Which came first, God's desire to have the Israelites commit genocide against the people already living in the Promised Land, or the Israelites' desire to possess the Promised Land and eliminate all the people who stand in their way? Did God actually command this kind of slaughter, or did the Israelites simply tell this story to excuse what they wanted to do or what they had already done?

I suggest it is the latter. The Israelites had a desire to defend or an action to excuse, and they invented this story to do it. The story serves because it legitimates the grounds of both the landgrab and the slaughter. First, it tells the Israelites the land is theirs by "inheritance," the implication being that the land has always been theirs: the Hebrews are not stealing land; they are recovering it. The Canaanites, the Perizzites, the Hivites, and the Jebusites never belonged on the land in the first place, so any claim they might make to the land (say that they've been living on it for centuries) is a nonstarter. Second, the story is careful to frame the Canaanites, Perizzites, Hivites, and Jebusites as "other." In fact, the text represents them as a contagion that must be wiped out lest it infect the people Israel with non-Israelite ideas.

This is what the stories of the mind do: they annex reality and reconfigure it in service to identity, whether that identity is one of statehood, peoplehood, or selfhood. Whatever does not suit the needs of these identities must be excised or subordinated. Sure, this is an extreme example, and not all stories of the mind are quite so naked in their application of power, nor in their dehumanization of the "other." Yet, the frightening fact is that the divisive and alienating principle at work in this Bible narrative is also at work in the mind's most basic acts of perception and knowledge production.

A few years ago I attended a seminar at Vanderbilt University on free will. The speaker raised all kinds of questions regarding the notion of free will and told us about a number of psychological experiments that cast doubt on the notion of free will. The one that struck me the most was a variant on a comedy routine often used on Drew Carey's improvisational comedy show *Whose Line Is It Anyway?*

On the show, one comic would stand with his arms clasped behind his back and face a table on which were placed a variety of objects: glasses of water, pieces of pie—things that would make a mess when used improperly. A second comic would stand behind the first and place his arms under the arms of the first comic, in effect becoming the first comic's hands and arms. Then the second comic would use his hands and arms to do things as if they were the hands and arms of the first comic. It was always very funny and very messy.

In the seminar version of this skit, the setup was the same with two changes. First, both people were wearing identical white lab coats so that the functioning arms of the second person looked just like the nonfunctioning arms of the first person. Second, as the second person began to manipulate the objects

what is true over information that challenges those notions. In other words, believing is seeing. Everyone suffers from this, and there is no escaping it. But, if you know you have it—and you do—you can begin to question your assumptions and the "facts" that back them up.

This bias comes up all the time in classes I teach on religion. Here is an actual conversation I had with a student recently. It is just one example of many that occur each semester.

> Student: "I can prove the Qur'an isn't the word of God."
> Me: "Really, how can you do that?"
> Student: "Because the Qur'an says God has no son, but God does have a son, and God wouldn't lie. The Qur'an denies God has a son; hence, it lies and cannot be the word of God."
> Me: "How do you know God has a son?"
> Student: "It is in the Bible."
> Me: "How do you know the Bible is true?"
> Student: "Because it tells us God had a son."

If this makes you smile, please stop. This isn't cute or funny. It is an all-too-common example of the blindness that marks the mind and defines the self. It is sad. And don't think I hear this kind of thinking from a certain kind of Christian only.

Years ago, I taught graduate-level religion classes at a private college in Florida. One semester I had two Hasidic Jews in my comparative religion class. The conversation turned to dinosaurs one day, and these two young men explained to the class that dinosaurs never existed. When God created the world less than 6,000 years ago, God created the bones of dinosaurs, made them appear to be millions of years old, and then buried them in the earth where scientists would find them thousands of years later. Why would God do this? To test our faith. Who are you going to believe: science or God? These young men opted for God.

I can't blame them for their choice. It is the only one they could make given the world from which they came and in which they choose to remain. I'm not telling you this story to suggest I am superior to people who think this way, but to suggest to you that we all think this way: we all rely on the opinions of others when those opinions support the biases we already carry.

For example, you trust your doctor, or your chiropractor, or you clergyperson, or your college professor, or your guru, or your parents, or your neighbor, or some "friend" you have never met except on Facebook who tells you that eating large hot fudge sundaes every night is only fattening if you eat them before 9:00 p.m. central time. Just so we are clear, this last opinion is not true, and that person is no longer my friend on Facebook.

This is how the mind works. It isn't logical, but it is practical; and while most of the time we lead fairly rational lives, there are times when we are trapped in irrational notions that make no sense in any setting other than the closed box in which we and those who think like us live. This is why I prefer to get my "news" from MSNBC while you may prefer to get yours from Fox. It is often not the same news.

Not too long ago, Ed Shultz of MSNBC reported that when Texas governor Rick Perry, a candidate for president of the United States in 2012, said that there is a "black cloud that hangs over America," he was referring to President Barack Obama. Wow! How racist is that!?! I knew those right-wing Texans were evil!

But wait. Flip over to Fox and you will discover that what Governor Perry actually said was this, "That big black cloud that hangs over America, that debt is so monstrous." Grammar aside, it is clear that no reference to President Obama was intended; the black cloud was the debt.

Was Ed Shultz deliberately misleading me? Maybe, but more likely he was a victim of confirmation bias. He "knew" what Governor Perry would say and then heard him say it even though he never said it at all.

A few days later on NPR's talk show *On Point* Shultz's misread of the Perry comment came up, and a caller phoned in to defend Ed Shultz with a lengthy exposé on the racial overtones of how the words *black* and *white* are used in this country: *black* is always negative and scary; *white* is always positive and welcoming. This doesn't always apply, of course: the KKK wore white sheets and *Walker, Texas Ranger* always wore a black cowboy hat, but these are the exceptions that prove the rule.

I'm not going to defend the use of "black" and "white" in American discourse, but the caller who lectured us about it was suffering from the same confirmation bias as Ed Shultz. It is everywhere.

Worse, it is often invisible. And it is precisely these invisible biases that are often the most dangerous. But this is where writing as a spiritual practice comes in. You can, through various writing exercises (some of which you will find in this chapter), confront the biases in your worldview, and your "story-verse." You can, again through writing, come to recognize your biases and, if you cannot free yourself from them completely, you can at least become aware of them, and so begin to question, to unsettle, the stories that shape your perception of life. We started to explore this in the previous exercise, so now let's take it a bit deeper.

Bye-Bye Bias, Part 1

Make a list of five of your most cherished opinions. Here are some examples:

America is the greatest country in the world.

Jews are God's chosen people.

Global warming is a hoax.

God exists and cares about you.

Pee-wee Herman was framed.

Write a one-page defense of your beliefs. Be clear, concise, and specific. Back up your opinion with facts, or at least back them up with other opinions you believe to be facts. Imagine you are writing to someone you care about, hoping to convince him or her of the rightness of your position. Don't explain why you believe as you do. Simply make what you believe as clear as possible.

Now go back and write another set of essays on why you believe as you do. You've already set forth the facts, so there is no need to repeat them. The goal of this essay isn't to convince someone why what you believe to be true is true, but to explain why you think this way. Is there something in your past that led you to think this way? What benefit do you derive from thinking this way? What feelings does this belief generate in you? Why do you value these feelings over others?

This exercise is a variation of The Work, a system of self-exploration and liberation developed by Byron Katie. The goal is to give you a glimpse into your own confirmation bias. As Byron Katie says on her website (www.thework.com):

> I discovered that when I believed my thoughts, I suffered, but that when I didn't believe them, I didn't suffer, and that this is true for every human being. Freedom is as simple as that. I found that suffering is optional. I found a joy within me that has never disappeared, not for a single moment. That joy is in everyone, always.

You believe in your thoughts—the stories you tell yourself and others about yourself and others—because of confirmation bias. You believe in your thoughts and stories because not believing in them is more frightening than believing in them. You believe in your thoughts and stories because without them you would be nobody, and nobody wants to be nobody. And yet discovering that you are nobody is exactly what needs to happen when we write to open the mind.

Bye-Bye Bias, Part 2

Having written a compelling argument for your biases, and having explored why you may believe what you believe, reverse these "truths" and write just as compellingly about the opposite opinion. Find as many facts to defend what you don't believe as you found to defend what you do believe.

The point of this exercise isn't difficult to uncover: what we call truth in the dimension of mind is simply that which supports our confirmation bias and in doing so brings comfort to us by supporting the world in which we imagine we live. To be blunt: truth from the perspective of mind is simply sacred opinion.

Sacred opinion is the subject of Charles P. Pierce's book *The American Way of Idiocy*. According to Pierce, something becomes a matter of sacred opinion when (1) it sells lots of books or ranks high in some other poll or rating system; (2) it is proclaimed loudly, insistently, and without nuance; and (3) enough people believe it to convince other people that they should believe it, too.[1] Truth, in other words, is manufactured.

The point is that you entertain lots of crazy ideas for no other reason than you don't think the people who passed them on to you are crazy. Fair enough. You've been warned. The real concern when it comes to writing as a spiritual practice is with the crazy ideas you cherish and that you use to define yourself and to shape the life you live. And the craziest idea you have is that you exist at all.

Perhaps that is going too far. Of course you exist; after all, you are reading this book. But the *you* you think you are isn't the *you* you really are. The *you* you think you are is a product of the stories you tell yourself and others about yourself. Too often spiritual writing is designed to maintain those stories, or, if they must be changed, to do so with the minimum amount of damage being done to the overall story of *you* to which you are attached. Writing as a spiritual practice attacks this kind of storytelling head-on.

Why should you do this? Because, to paraphrase Hamlet: there are more things in heaven and earth than are dreamt of in your philosophy. By writing to unsettle bias, we may put one or two small holes in the veil of our preset perceptions, and perhaps get a glimpse of something unexpected, something that reawakens us to the dazzling miracle of life, or something that forever alters the way we see ourselves and each other.

THE IDEOLOGY OF LANGUAGE

Writing to unsettle bias, though, is just one way of writing to open the mind. A second method involves breaking down our use of language. Language, in many ways, constitutes the ultimate bias, because it is language that lies at the heart of consciousness. We cannot think without it. And yet, as we have seen, the words we use to give shape to our thoughts have a subtle influence on those thoughts. They permit some ideas while refusing others, permit some perceptions while locking others out. And we hardly ever notice that the world we experience has been changed.

Indeed, most of us, when we use a word, imagine that the word has a specific referent: a denotation, a stable, reliable meaning. We say "rose" and we mean "rose, because a rose is a rose is a rose." But the truth is that words really have no meaning that isn't socially constructed. A word in itself is simply a set of phonemes—a set of sounds. And the connection between those sounds and the meanings they carry is tenuous at best. While it is true that some words (like *rock* and *stone*) may reflect something of their referents' physical qualities, most words have no direct relationship to things at all.

Ferdinand de Saussure (1857–1913), the father of structural linguistics, developed a three-part system to explain words, or rather, the phenomenon of representation in language. Words, he said, are signifiers, that is, symbols that refer to things or concepts. The thing or concept referred to by a particular word is called the signified. But there is no real relationship between a signifier and its signified. This is why I can ask for a glass of water in America and then turn around and ask for *un vaso de agua* in Spain, or *un verre d'eau* in France, or *bru wo ippai kudasai* in Japan, and end up receiving a glass of water. What holds the signified and the signifier together is something called the sign. The sign doesn't really exist, at least not in a way that can be objectively measured. It is not a thing, but a set of usage conventions shaped by social, historical, and political factors.

Take the phrase *French fries*. I love French fries. They are salty, greasy, crisp, and hot, and they come in wonderful cardboard containers shaped vaguely like the newspaper hats I used to fold and wear as a kid. Fries are fantastic. What they aren't, however, is French. In fact, they're Belgian. Historical accounts suggest that Belgians were frying up thin strips of potato as early as the seventeenth century, and that it was the Belgians who introduced fried potatoes to the French. But it was the French who started selling fries (called *pommes frites* or *frites*) on the streets of Paris in pushcarts, and it was these Parisian pushcart vendors who introduced fries to American soldiers during World War I, and it was America that (thanks to Ray Kroc and McDonald's) spread fries throughout the world. So, sorry Belgium, the world got French fries.

The point here is that Romeo's beloved Juliet was largely wrong when she claimed that a rose by any other name would smell as sweet. Sure, the rose itself would not change, but try getting someone to stop and smell the crap-blossoms. Or try ordering *pommes frites* at your local Micky D's. The signifying relationship between words and their referents may be objectively arbitrary, but subjectively a whole array of influences comes into play to hold a word and its referent together. This is what Saussure meant by the term *sign*. It stands for the whole constellation of historical and political events and socioeconomic factors that come together to shape a name and make it stick. And this is what words really are. Not sounds, not concepts, but stories.

Definitions

Words are stories, and the dictionary is an encyclopedia. Crack open a word, look into its etymology, and you'll find a whole history: politics, war, economic booms and busts, cultural and intellectual paradigm shifts, and more. All of it is embedded in even the most mundane word. Take the word *jury*, for example. *Jury* has its root in French, as do *indict* and *verdict*. Why? Because when William the Conqueror, the duke of Normandy, invaded England in 1066, he subjugated the Anglo-Saxons living there and established French (really Anglo-Norman) as the language of the aristocracy, forcing English (Old English, that is) underground. Meanwhile, the ruling bodies of government, including the courts, adopted Anglo-Norman as the language of politics and law. So the class divisions created between Anglo-Saxons and Anglo-Normans over a millennium ago remain at work in our language today.

The same can be said of any word in any language. Each contains an entire history. And more. Each word is equally influenced by its contemporary usage, by the set of conventions that govern where and when and how we may say a word. But while, on the one hand, these facts speak to the richness of language, on the other, they suggest that language can lock us into a set of biases and perceptual limitations that we may not even be aware of.

Which brings us to our prompt. Designed as a parlor game by those wily avant-garde surrealists, this prompt attempts to undermine the biases and limitations embedded in language by unsettling the one-to-one link between a word and its meaning. The game is called, simply, Definitions.

The game is played best with a partner, or in a group, so step one is to find yourself a friend or two (or more) to play with. Once you have gathered your group, make sure everyone has a pen or pencil and a sheet of paper, and ask everyone to sit together in a circle. When everyone is seated comfortably, you are ready to play. Here's how:

1. On a sheet of paper, each player should write a list of abstract nouns, words like *love*, *loss*, *soul*, *self*, *God*, *pain*, *bliss*, *holiness*, and so on. The nouns should be flush with the right margin, and only one noun should appear on any line. It is often a good idea to skip a line or two between nouns.

2. Add the verb *is* next to each abstract noun on your list. Leave a fair amount of space between the noun and the verb, so that all the *is* verbs line up vertically.

3. Fold the paper over so that all the nouns are covered, but the word *is* is still visible. Then, hand the paper to the person sitting to your left.

4. You should now be staring at a sheet of paper covered in *is*. Select one *is* and write the image that comes to your mind. The image should be as specific as possible. Use concrete nouns and verbs this time, and allow the image to be as complex

or simple as you like. For example: "a bridge collapsing in the orange rays of sunset," "a frog lapping flies in a pool at dusk." Even the absurd is acceptable: "a choir of knives," "a racehorse cantata."

5. Once you have written your image, pass the paper again to the person to your left. Continue writing and passing on the pages until each page full of *is* is filled with images. Then, unfold the pages, and read the new definitions you have created.

Some of the definitions you discover in this exercise may be funny, others merely odd. But some will be oddly appropriate, and some of them may stick with you, catching in your mind so that you never imagine love, loss, soul, self, God, pain, bliss, or holiness quite the same way ever again.

It is the storied nature of words that makes them so powerful. Words can conjure anything, whether real or imaginary. And it is often the most imaginary words that carry the greatest power. Take the word *God*, for example. People are willing to torture and be tortured because of the word *God*; they kill and are killed because of it. And yet there is no reason outside the world of words to believe that *God* refers to anything beyond its own literary context.

For instance, several years ago I was wandering through a Christian rock concert held at Centennial Park in Nashville, Tennessee. I love both Christian rock and Christian kitsch, and this gathering was teeming with both. As I wandered through the stalls looking at the cool T-shirts praising Jesus and affirming the fact that the T-shirt wearer is not hell-bound, I heard one of the concert MCs take the mic:

"Is this a great gathering or what? Hallelujah! Praise Jesus!"

The crowd responded enthusiastically, and I listened more attentively, ready to enjoy what is always a moving celebration of God. But rather than praise Christ, the MC challenged the crowd:

"How many of you are willing to kill for Christ?"

Did I hear that right? Being willing to die for Christ (or Yahweh or Allah, for that matter) is pretty standard fare for many religious people, but to "kill for Christ" was something I had not heard at a concert. I would have insisted I had misheard the speaker, had he not repeated it:

"How many of you are willing to kill for Christ?"

The crowd shouted their willingness to commit homicide, and I walked briskly away. It is fine with me if people want to die for their God, but when it comes to killing for God, I start to get nervous. After all, I'm Jewish, and history suggests that when a people decides to kill for its God, it is often *my* people who end up dying.

My intent here isn't to mock Christianity, or to imply that Christians are any more susceptible to killing for God than any other believers. What I want to point out is that the God so many of us are willing to kill for only exists in the realm of words.

Imagine the response of the crowd if the MC had said, "How many of you are willing to kill for Krishna?" I doubt he would have gotten a single volunteer. Yet both Christ and Krishna are God in their respective contexts. My point is that the word *God* has no external referent outside of human literature, outside the stories we tell about God. We cannot point to an object and say: "This thing, or this class of things, is God," at least not the way we can with trees, cats, or French fries. Indeed, the only way we can define or explain God is to refer to holy books, powerful sermons, or some other text or teaching that is itself made up of words.

There's an important lesson here. Words, or rather stories, shape reality—or to put it more accurately, they so powerfully shape the human perception of reality that they influence all our attempts to comprehend and interact with reality. Consider again the bias hidden in the connotations surrounding the words *black* and *white*. The radio caller who observed these biases wasn't wrong, though his attempt to link them to Rick Perry's speech may have been misguided. Nevertheless, his observation is correct. To illustrate, here's a few selections from *Merriam-Webster's Dictionary*:

> white: ... marked by upright fairness <that's mighty *white* of you> ... free from spot or blemish ... free from moral impurity: INNOCENT: marked by the wearing of white by the woman as a symbol of purity <a *white* wedding>: ... not intended to cause harm <a *white* lie> ...

> black: ... DIRTY, SOILED <hands *black* with grime> ... characterized by the absence of light <a *black* night> ... thoroughly sinister or evil: WICKED <a *black* deed> ... indicative of condemnation or discredit <got a *black* mark [on his record] for being late> ... connected with or invoking the supernatural, especially the devil <*black* magic> ... very sad, gloomy, or calamitous <*black* despair> ... marked by the occurrence of disaster <*Black* Friday> ... characterized by hostility <*black* resentment filled his heart> ... grim, distorted, or grotesque <*black* humor>

Of course, these examples don't prove that the English language is fundamentally racist. Some of these definitions and usages go back a long way, and may have been in place well before Europeans began to refer to some dark-skinned people as black. But that's just the point. By using the word *black* to describe people of African descent, English-speaking colonial cultures created (whether consciously or unconsciously) an intrinsic link between these people and a host of preexisting negative connotations. Creating this link is, of course, just one more move in dehumanizing people of color, and thus excusing and justifying the viciousness of colonization and slavery.

Our language today is full of words and phrases like this, idioms that construct and maintain unequal power relations. Consider the commonplace idiom *you guys.* According to *Webster's,* I can use the phrase *you guys* as a gender-neutral term. I can use it, for example, to address my classes, to address an entire room full of young men and women. And yet, in doing so, I erase from existence each and every young woman in the room. We hardly ever notice we are doing this kind of thing. Our language is so engrained, its usage so seemingly natural, that we typically speak (and think and write) without really being aware of what it is we are saying.

This is where, once again, writing as a spiritual practice must step in. Just as we have done with bias, so must we do with language. We must write against it, write in ways designed to reveal its coded inequalities, its recapitulation of the status quo. And we must go further. We must write to unsettle the illusory one-to-one relationship between words and meaning, because it is here, in this made-up relationship, that our consciousness, our compassion, and our infinite imagination are trapped.

Writing Against Language: The Vorpal Blade

The title of this prompt comes from Lewis Carroll's poem "Jabberwocky," a wonderfully weird bit of nonsense verse made up almost entirely of invented words:

> 'Twas brillig, and the slithy toves
> Did gyre and gimble in the wabe;
> All mimsy were the borogoves,
> And the mome raths outgrabe.

> "Beware the Jabberwock, my son
> The jaws that bite, the claws that catch!

Beware the Jubjub bird, and shun
The frumious Bandersnatch!"

He took his vorpal sword in hand;
Long time the manxome foe he sought—
So rested he by the Tumtum tree,
And stood awhile in thought.

And, as in uffish thought he stood,
The Jabberwock, with eyes of flame,
Came whiffling through the tulgey wood,
And burbled as it came!

One, two! One, two! And through and through
The vorpal blade went snicker-snack!
He left it dead, and with its head
He went galumphing back.

"And hast thou slain the Jabberwock?
Come to my arms, my beamish boy!
O frabjous day! Callooh! Callay!"
He chortled in his joy.

'Twas brillig, and the slithy toves
Did gyre and gimble in the wabe;
All mimsy were the borogoves,
And the mome raths outgrabe.

What's fun about this poem is that, despite its bizarre
vocabulary, the plot of the poem is nevertheless
perfectly intelligible (with the exception of the first and
last stanzas). We do not need to know, for example,
precisely what a "bandersnatch" is to interpret the word
as referring to some rather frightening beast. Context
clues provide all the meaning necessary. And yet, the
words themselves are fascinating, and many, many
literary critics and historians (not to mention fans) have

tried to guess their meanings and their origins. Carroll himself left commentary, but it is often contradictory, and frequently ridiculous, a continuation of the poem's play with meaning and meaninglessness. For our purposes, though, the important thing is this: language is infinitely malleable. We can, if we want, make meaning from nonsense. We can invent words, splice them together, scramble them up, and still communicate. That is the goal of this prompt, to push language to the breaking point, to construct new words with new histories and new meanings, and then write with them and discover what they say.

Inventing new words is not easy. Well, actually, it is ... once you get started. But that's the tricky bit: starting, escaping the pull of the (on average) 20,000 English words already rattling around in your head. For help, we can turn to Carroll.

1. Portmanteau words: combine two or more words to make a new word. For example, Slithy is a combination of lithe and slimy; mimsy combines flimsy and miserable.
2. Verbing: take a noun and change the word ending to make it a verb. To gimble, as Carroll explains, is to make small holes as with a gimlet (a hand drill).
3. Onomatopoeia: invent new words based on sound. The "Jubjub bird," for instance, may have been named for its distinctive (imaginary) call.
4. Deforming: select phonemes common to a few loosely related words, and then add prefixes or suffixes. Uffish, says Carroll, derives from rough, gruff, and huffy.
5. Etymological borrowing: take words from the history of English and revamp them as

contemporary. For instance: *outgribe* (again, according to Carroll) derives from the old verb *grike*, "to shriek." You might also try this with languages other than English—which would save you the trouble of having to research Old and Middle English vocabulary.

6. Pure nonsense: find a sound you like, and imagine a meaning. Any meaning. A *tove*, Humpty Dumpty tells us, is something like a badger, lizard, and corkscrew all at once.

Once you have invented a dozen or so new words, which is rewarding in its own right, you can begin to experiment with them. You might write a simple scene or short poem using as many of the words as possible. You might write them into a dialogue, or actually work them into real-life conversations. The more words you invent, the more you can do with them. The goal, however, is simply to play, to write and speak joyous nonsense and take pleasure in making meaning from meaninglessness. Or vice versa.

While this exercise can be playful and fun, it is also deadly serious. When you realize you can make up words, you begin to realize that all words are made up. And when you realize that all words are made up it is more and more difficult to die for them, let alone kill for them.

FOR LOVE OF MAN AND SUPERMAN

If I am asked to complete the sentence "Love is," my first thoughts are well-worn clichés: "Love is a two-way street; love is a many-splendored thing." If asked to define love, I am most likely to say something like: "an intimate, trusting relationship between two people." This is fine, as far as it goes. But it doesn't go very far. What of the love that is "like branches floating in the river," or love that is "like a building on fire"? What of "penguin dust" love, or "limousine eyelash" love? Sure, these may seem like ridiculous phrases, but isn't love, at its best, joyously ridiculous? Why *can't* love be a limousine eyelash? The only thing standing in its way is language, and our habitual, reflexive submission to the tyranny of *making sense*.

When writing to open the mind we must dare to stop making sense. We must embrace the ridiculous, the impossible, and the absurd. Consider Superman, for example. Yes, Superman. Strange visitor from another planet, who came to Earth with powers and abilities far beyond those of mortal men. Superman, who can change the course of mighty rivers, bend steel in his bare hands, and who, disguised as Clark Kent, mild-mannered reporter for a major metropolitan newspaper, fights a never-ending battle for truth, justice, and the American way.

Superman, we know, is fiction. A character put together by Jerry Siegel and Joe Shuster in 1932 that first appeared in *Action Comics* #1 in 1938. Since then, though, Superman has grown. He has leapt, not over tall buildings, but across media, from comic books to radio to television to film to video games. And he has leapt across dimensions, from the two-dimensional universe of media to the three-dimensional universe of action figures, board games, playing cards, lunchboxes, T-shirts, collectible models, and costumes. Most important, he has leapt across narratives, from the fictional narratives of his origins to the very real narratives of American national identity. Superman is today an indelible part of America's self-image, standing not just for American power, but also for our core cultural values, for all that is best in us. He is the defender of the weak, the enemy of tyrants. He has become the symbol, in many ways, of the nation we want to be.

His impact goes beyond the symbolic. Superman, along with his buddies in the Justice Society, helped inspire America to join the fight against Nazi Germany, battling Hitler on paper long before American troops set foot in the battlefields of Europe.

As the war continued, the U.S. Army, in partnership with National Periodical Publications, better known today as DC Comics, printed hundreds of thousands of Superman comics, distributing them to GIs to keep up morale and, what is more, to improve literacy. These comics helped soldiers who had little or no education learn to read, so they could better understand the Army manuals designed to aid them in operating and maintaining complex military equipment. Of course, the GIs also handed out the comics to kids in war-torn countries as a gesture of American goodwill.

Superman shaped the American psyche, and was in turn shaped by it. The stories we tell shape our reality, even when they are pure fantasy. And sometimes, in embracing the fantastic, in pushing our stories beyond what is merely possible, what is sensible, we may find ourselves revising reality for the better. At the very least, though, in embracing the fantastic and absurd, we liberate ourselves from the strictures of the real as we know it, as it has been shaped for us by the stories embedded in our culture and in our language. And we become free to tell new stories of our own.

I, Superhero

Without thinking, answer this question: What super power would you want if you could have any super power at all? Now sit and write about why you would want that power and what you would do with it. What does your fantasy power say about the "you" you imagine yourself to be without this power?

Alter Ego

Without thinking, answer these questions: How would you hide your super power from the world? What would your alter ego be like? How does this alter ego compare to the "you" you imagine yourself to be right now, the "you" that is neither a superhero or an alter ego?

Calling Dr. Freud, Calling Dr. Freud

Not all superheroes have alter egos. The Fantastic Four and the X-Men, for example, don't bother to hide their tights by donning the costumes of ordinary folk. They are who they are and make no attempt to hide who they are. So why did you choose an alter ego? Why are you hiding your powers? Why can't you just be who you are? What are you worried about?

If you got into this exercise and answered these questions without too much thought you were living a fantasy. Chances are no matter how angry you get you aren't going to grow into a huge green monster and set about destroying your neighborhood shouting, "Puny humans! Hulk will smash!" And yet if the exercise caught your attention you did something very much like it. You became someone else and called him or her yourself.

This is what writing to open the mind is all about: using words to revise reality, and in so doing realize that reality is a linguistic construct.

Surprisingly, the opening story of creation in the book of Genesis agrees. Before God creates anything what did exist was *tohu v'vohu*, chaotic and unformed (Genesis 1:2). God doesn't subdue or slay chaos, God only calls order out of it: "And God said ..." God speaks and the world comes into being—holy abracadabra! According to the Bible the world that you and I inhabit is nothing more than a linguistic creation. The world is nothing more than God's words, and beneath those words continues the wildness of *tohu v'vohu*. Is it any wonder that crazy things happen? Is it any wonder that in a world where matter is made up of words, words matter?

Sticks and Stones

The phrase "Sticks and stones may break my bones, but names will never hurt me" is mere bravado. Names always hurt. Write about a time when you were hurt by the names you were called. Make a list of the names you are still called, and the hurtful names you call yourself. Why do these names still carry emotional weight? Why do you still carry them around and respond to them?

YOU WHO

Language is a kind of magic: it casts a spell. Indeed, as we grow up and learn to use language properly, one of the first things we have to learn is how to spell, literally how to cast letters to make words in order to make worlds and meaning. It isn't an accident that the word *spell* has both meanings. Writing as a spiritual practice helps us break the spell of language.

As we have seen, this can be done by writing against bias, by writing against language, and by writing against sense, but perhaps the most powerful act of breaking the spell of language is writing against the self.

Writing against the self is writing to open the mind, and it works by unsettling and revising the story of your self. You are the stories you tell, especially the stories you tell about yourself. The self you are is the self you remember, but most of those memories are highly edited. Hardly anyone remembers things exactly as they happened. The *you* you imagine yourself to be is a construct, a character in a drama you create to give continuity to your life. Because you assume the *you* you were at age eight is the *you* you were at age eighteen and the *you* you are today, you have to tell a story that links all these yous (and dozens more) into a seamless whole. But in what sense is this true?

Most of the cells in your body today didn't exist seven years ago; the thoughts you had this morning are not the same as the thoughts you had a decade ago; you don't react emotionally to the world today as you did when you were seven years old, so what is this *you* you keep harping on? It is the story: "When I was six ...; A few years ago, I ...; Just yesterday I ..." Story.

I once met a man on an airplane who told me that he invented new identities for himself every time he flew. If someone asked him who he was and what he did, he would invent a new name and career. He didn't use these false identities to take advantage of anyone, but simply to entertain himself at others' expense. Of course, he could have been making this up at my expense also, so when he asked me about who I was and what I did I told him my name was Hank and that I worked as a garbage man, something I had wanted to do when I was a toddler.

The difference between the self I invented on the plane and the self I invent right now is that I was conscious of inventing my airplane self while I maintain the conceit that the self I take myself to be at this moment is in fact the self I am. But this is just a conceit.

So who are you really? You don't know. Who am I really? I don't know. And not knowing is just fine, at least as long as you don't insist things be otherwise. The only time not knowing becomes a problem is when you insist you must know.

Earlier we spoke about your original face, the face you had before your parents were born. This phrase comes from a Zen Buddhist koan. A koan is a puzzle that you turn around and around in your mind until it drives you out of that mind and into no-mind; out of the storied self and into the unstoried Self. The Zen master confronts you with this koan and demands an answer: Show me your face before your parents were born!

You can't. You didn't have one. While this seems straightforward enough, when I offered that bit of logic to a Zen master confronting me with that koan, he said, "Fine. Show me your face when your parents were born." Sticking with my logic I answered in the same vein: "I didn't yet have a face when my parents were born." My teacher was as persistent in his questioning as I was in my answers: "Fine! Show me your face now!"

Then it hit me. I didn't have a face now either. I could have made a face; I could have stuck my tongue out at him and pretended that irreverence was the same as enlightenment, hoping that he was as easily fooled by cleverness as I was, but even as this thought crossed my mind I knew it was a lie. Making a face wasn't the same as having one. All I could do was make faces. I couldn't find the one I had. Why? Because I didn't and don't have one.

Zen master Lin-Chi (Rinzai in Japanese), after whom the Rinzai school of Zen Buddhism is named, spoke of the enlightened person as being "a person of no rank." This is a person who is free from notions of success and failure, winning and losing, being this and not that or being that and not this. Being a person of no rank isn't being humble or arrogant; it doesn't make you a pauper or a tycoon; it frees you from all that. Of course, if you call yourself a "person of no rank" then "person of no rank" becomes a rank and you are no more enlightened than anyone else.

In his poem titled "Poetry," the Chilean poet Pablo Neruda (1904–1973) tells us that poetry came to him when he was "without a face." And because he was without a face he could say from where poetry came. Wang Wei, a T'ang Dynasty (618–907) Chinese poet, tells us that your face, the face you wear in public, tells you who you were, but never who you are. And Emily Dickinson celebrates the faceless in her poem, "I'm Nobody":

> *I'm nobody! Who are you?*
> *Are you—Nobody—too?*
> *Then there's a pair of us!*
> *Don't tell!*
> *they'd banish us—you know.*
>
> *How dreary—to be—Somebody!*
> *How public—like a Frog—*
> *To tell one's name—the livelong June—*
> *To an admiring Bog!*

Let's be very careful here. There are two types of facelessness in the world; one of them enslaves, the other liberates. There have been and continue to be entire peoples who remain faceless in the eyes of their occupiers. There have been and continue to be people whom society refuses to see, or if it does see them insists that they remain faceless. This is not the facelessness that liberates. This is not the facelessness of Neruda, Wang Wei, and Emily Dickinson. This is a facelessness that some stories we tell impose on some people we tell them about. These people need their faces returned, and any story you tell that denies them their face should cease to be told.

LIVING ANOTHER'S STORY

Before moving on to liberate ourselves from our faces, let's explore a bit more of how we can be forced to deny our face and wear the masks others place on us.

Years ago I was teaching at a Jewish educational conference when a woman asked if she could join me in the cafeteria for lunch. We went through the line, got our food, and sat at a long table to eat. Once we had made a bit of small talk, she shifted the conversation to the reason she wanted to talk with me.

"My parents named me after my father's sister. She was killed in Dachau. When I was born my dad believed that I was his sister reincarnated. They gave me her name, insisted that I like the foods she liked, wear the colors she wore, and cultivate the hobbies and interests she had loved. They didn't just give me her name; they gave me her life. I have lived as this dead woman my entire life, but now my parents are dead, and I want to be myself, but I don't know who that is or if I can. Or even if I should. I mean, the Nazis killed her, who am I to kill her again?"

I had no idea how to respond to this woman. For some reason I asked her how old she was. She was forty-nine.

"Well, then, that explains it," I said, having no idea what I was talking about.

She stared at me inquisitively. I stared back blankly. That explains what, I thought. And then I knew:

In the book of Leviticus the Torah speaks of a Jubilee year. Every seven years the land is to lay fallow in order to rejuvenate itself. And every seven cycles of seven years the entire culture is to do the same. All land bought and sold during the prior half century is returned to its original owners or their descendants, all slaves are freed, and all debts are forgiven: "And you shall hallow the fiftieth year and all debts shall be forgiven and all ancestral holdings restored" (Leviticus 25:10; my translation). I explained this to my lunch partner and said:

"So you had a debt to your parents and maybe your aunt. You were, in a sense, indebted to her memory. But that is ending now. You've paid that debt, and now you are free. This is your personal Jubilee year, your personal seventh cycle of seven years. This is the year in which you are released. You can choose to be who you were, or you can choose to be who you are."

"But who am I?"

"No one can tell you that. Not your dad, not your mom, not your aunt—no one. You have to invent that for yourself."

"Invent it? Don't you mean discover it?"

"No," I said, "invent it. Discovering yourself implies there is a fixed self out there that is you, and your parents were keeping you from finding it. There isn't, and they weren't. We are not born with a fixed self, but with the capacity to create selves. When we are young we do this all the time, but over time we settle for one self or another and pretend this is who we are rather than who have simply settled into being. We are who we create ourselves to be."

"But how do I do that?"

"The same way your parents did. They told you a story about your aunt and they asked you or forced you to conform to it. Now you are free to tell new stories about yourself."

"Like?"

"Like how you were a loving and dutiful daughter who went along with her parents' story and became the girl they wanted—the murdered sister they lost—and who has now come to the end of that duty and is free to invent a new self for the next seven-year cycle."

"I can do that?"

"You may do it," I said. "Whether or not you can is completely up to you."

I never saw this woman again. I don't know what she did with what I said, but I never forgot that I said it. The truth of what I said to her is compelling to me. Not that I have freed myself from all my parental conditioning—far from it—but that I know that who I am is the story I tell, and if I wish to be different I must tell a different story.

Who Am I?

Imagine the person you were raised to be is actually modeled on somebody else. It may not matter who; it just isn't the real you: the you you imagine yourself to be when you are lying alone with your thoughts in bed, the you you would be if you weren't the you you are.

Now imagine that you are entering your personal Jubilee. You are being freed from the you you were, freed to be the you you wish you were.

What would your name be? What would you love? Whom would you love? What would you do to earn a living? How would you spend your time? Your money?

Write a short essay introducing yourself. Tell us everything we need to know if we are to know this new you deeply.

Now do it again, but this time assume this new you is also a false you. If this were not you either, who would you be? Tell us about this person. Then do it again and again until you reach a point where you cannot imagine being anyone else. This last you still isn't you, but by now you know that you are never the story you tell.

The goal of writing as a spiritual practice is to free yourself from your story. The story may be about how you were addicted to pain medication and with the help of Jesus Christ, Twelve Steps, Scientology, or Meher Baba you were cured of your addiction and liberated to be your true self, which is the self now defined by whomever you listen to in whatever system you have taken refuge in.

This isn't bad. This isn't wrong. Whatever works to get you clean is fine by me. I've been there; I know. All I am saying is that this kind of writing isn't about ending the self but substituting one idea of self for another: the addicted self for the free self. Writing as a spiritual practice simply explodes the notion of self altogether by making it painfully clear that the self is a story and nothing more.

Why is this desirable? Because once you know your self is a story, you can change it more easily. As long as you imagine that you are someone or other—a Christian, a Jew, a Muslim, a Hindu, a Buddhist, a vegetarian, a Rastafarian, or whatever—you have to either justify who you are or justify why you are rejecting who you are in order to become someone else.

For example, I'm Jewish, not only biologically but also professionally. I teach Judaism and American Jewish literature. Yet I am not happy being boxed in by that label. Being Jewish comes with all kinds of baggage that I don't want to schlep around. I don't believe in a God who chooses people, yet being Jewish is rooted in being chosen. I don't believe that God dabbles in real estate, and yet Judaism is rooted in the Promised Land. I don't believe Torah was dictated to Moses by God, yet Judaism is rooted in Torah as revelation. So am I Jewish or not?

I say I am, and I make meaning out of the stories of Judaism and of my being Jewish even if it isn't the same meaning that others who lay claim to these stories make. But being Jewish isn't my only story. Deeper than my being Jewish is my being human, and deeper than my being human is my being God, although not all of God. I am free to have all these stories because I know everything is story, and story is imagined. And what is imagined can be reimagined—in any way we choose.

The prompts that follow will help you toward such reimagining. They will challenge you to confront your biases, to remake the language that shapes your perceptions, and to retell the story of your self. In doing so, you turn the spiral of the five worlds outward from the dimension of mind and into the dimension of soul, liberating yourself from the stories of division and alienation that are the mind's favorite fictions.

My Destiny

Somewhere between one-quarter and one-third of all Americans read their daily horoscope. You may be one of them, or you may not. Believing in astrology is not necessary for this exercise. Playing with horoscopes is.

Pick up two copies of today's newspaper and put them aside to be used later. Wait until evening when the most active part of your day has ended, then take one copy of the newspaper and open it to the horoscope section. Do not read your horoscope. If you can't help yourself, ask a friend to get the newspapers and set this exercise up for you. Cut out each horoscope but leave off the zodiac sign to which it belongs. You should end up with twelve outlooks without the labels Taurus, Aquarius, Cancer, and so on. Shuffle the twelve slips of paper in a bag or box, and pull one out at random. Read it carefully and think about your day. Write a short biography of your day from the perspective of this horoscope, focusing on its accuracy. Do the same thing with a second one, and then a third, and continue until all twelve have been explored.

Review all twelve and pick the one you like the best, the one that seems the truest and most compelling to you. Then take the other copy of the newspaper, open it to the horoscope page and see which zodiac sign you preferred. Chances are it wasn't the sign assigned to you by your birth date. If it was and you don't currently believe in astrology, you might want to change you mind. If it wasn't you might begin to think about how you are the story you tell and how the story you tell is shaped by ideas you may not even believe in.

The Name Game

Lots of people take their names—given and chosen— very seriously. They peruse name dictionaries to find out the derivation of their name, and may check out "your name is your destiny" books to see the implications of their name. None of these insights is more or less true than any others, and they may make for a good story. A good story is what having a name is all about.

We know that stories always link back to self. The Self has no story. Knowing your name is part of knowing your story, and knowing the story of your name is another chapter of that story. When we work with writing as a spiritual practice we are not opposed to story, we just want to be clear that it is story. Knowing that your story is a story leads to the freedom associated with both spiritual and psychological maturity. What is psychotherapy, after all, but the discovery of your story, and the realization that you can rewrite it so that it is a bit less fixated on self and a bit more open to Self? And what is spiritual practice if not the shattering of your story to reveal—if only for a moment—the unstoried Self behind it all?

You can't shatter your story directly, but you can become so aware of the storied nature of self as to not be enslaved to either story or self, and that will be quite enough.

One way to do this is to play with the story of your name in a manner quite different from those found in name books, both the dictionaries that tell you the history of your name and the *destinaries* that claim to reveal the future of those who bear it (I think I invented this word, and it is a good one).

Marc-Alain Ouaknin, a French professor and rabbi, has written a fascinating book called *Mysteries of the Alphabet: The Origins of Writing.* In the book Rabbi Oauknin introduces the idea of *archeography.*

Archeography, a word coined by Ouaknin, is the practice of analyzing and interpreting the meaning of words based not only on their etymological origins, but also on the objects the letters of the words symbolized in their earliest proto-Sinaitic form. For example, the English word *ax* is comprised of two letters, *a* and *x.* According to Rabbi Ouaknin, the English letter *a* in its earliest proto-Sinaitic form symbolized the head of an ox, and the letter *x* represented a skeleton. How does this lead to the English word *ax?* No one knows. That is where the story comes in: you are free to imagine a link.

For example, perhaps a primitive ax (called by whatever name) was used to kill and skin animals. One used the ax to kill the ox by chopping off its head, and then to flay the flesh from the dead animal, leaving only the skeleton. Hence the word *ox head skeleton* or, in English, *ax.* While this may make for less than rigorous science, it makes for a very rigorous story prompt.

None of this can be proven, and none of it matters. What matters is that Rabbi Ouaknin has provided us with a marvelous way of reading our names and telling a story.

Here is each letter of the English alphabet coupled with the object(s) Rabbi Ouaknin says lay in the letter's distant past:

A Head of an ox

B House

C Camel

D Door

E A human praying

F Nail, masthead, neck rest, pillow

G Two crossed swords

H Barrier, enclosure

I Hand, palm open

J Hand, palm open

K Palm of the hand

L Ox goad

M Water, river, waves

N Fish

O Eye

P Mouth

Q Ax, hatchet

R Head

S Tooth

T Cross, shield

U Nail, masthead, neck rest, pillow

V Nail, masthead, neck rest, pillow

W Nail, masthead, neck rest, pillow

X Tree, fishbone, skeleton

Y Hand with dot

Z Crossed swords (like G)

Write out your name archeographically and write a short exposition on what it means and what it says about you, your personality, and your life. Write in the third person as if you were an objective observer, an archeographologist, if you will.

Now do the same for significant others in your life. Compare your name with another's name and see what archeographical links you can find between the two of you. Do this with friends and see if you can spin a story of harmony. Do it with enemies and see if you can spin a story of disharmony. The more you discover about yourself and those close to you and the more clear you are that you are making all of this up in your mind the freer you will become from all the stories that define you.

Narrowing the Narrow Mind

One reason people go to therapists is to gain insight into their story. Another is that no one else will listen to them. Think about this: how long can you listen to a friend tell and retell her story before you are ready to scream, "Enough already! If you don't like your job—quit! If you want to lose ten pounds—skip dessert! Just stop with the drama for God's sake!"

Therapists don't do that. One reason they don't is because they are trained not to. Another reason is that they may genuinely believe that if they can get you to really hear your story you may get as bored with it as the rest of us, and begin to tell and live a different, and it is hoped, more healthy one. The third reason is that you pay them to listen. This is your fifty-minute hour; you paid for it; and if you want to repeat the same sad story over and over again, well, that is just what you are going to do, and the therapist had better sit there and look interested or you'll find some other therapist who will.

Good therapists, of course, won't put up with this, but there are many who will.

A good therapist will help you focus your story. A good friend can do this as well, and that is what this next exercise is about.

You may think your entire story is riveting, and for you it may be. But for a listener or reader, most of what you say is boring, tangential, and meaningless. If you are trying to be a sparkling personality, this can be quite devastating. But it can also be most liberating.

Narrowing the Narrow Mind is done with a partner. This should be someone you trust. The role of each partner in this exercise is to write his or her own piece and edit the other's.

Take fifteen minutes to write a short autobiography. Don't worry about details or grammar. Just write what you remember about the big touchstone events in your life, setting the stage, showing us what happened, and making it clear to the reader what these events felt like to you.

When the fifteen minutes are up, stop writing, and exchange papers. Read through your partner's essay and underline or highlight with a marker the one sentence that captures your attention more than all the others. Then hand the essay back, retrieve your own, and begin writing all over again starting with that one sentence.

Do this for another fifteen minutes. When the fifteen minutes are up, stop writing, and exchange papers once again. This time as you read your partner's essay highlight a different sentence, one that seems tangential to the essay's main focus. Then each of you retrieves your individual essay, and writes it again starting with that highlighted sentence.

You could do this exercise over and over again, with a new story emerging every time. The point? We are the stories we tell, and there is a different self being created by each story. Referencing examples from an elderly woman named Emma who attended one of my Path & Pen workshops, the Emma who told the story of her grandmother dying in her arms during a fire in the tenement is a frightened, superstitious woman, while the Emma who told the story of her dad and the perfume he surprised her mother with was someone else entirely. Which is the true Emma? There is no true Emma; there is only the Emma embedded in one tale or another.

Narrow mind identifies with one story or one collection of stories, and defines itself accordingly. These are the stories it tells over and over again to reinforce that identity. This is the identity that may become threatened if the story or the meaning one attaches to it is challenged.

The Three Garments of Self

According to Jewish tradition, the egoic I, mind, or self manifests in the world in three ways: through thought, word, and deed. These are called the three garments. Each garment has its own take on your story, and it is often insightful to hear them each articulated distinct from the other two.

Think of a scene from your own life, and write it out in bare-bones style.

Now retell the event three times, each time emphasizing one of the three garments. In the first version, focus on the thoughts you had when dealing with that moment of your life. Of course, you will have to imagine what they were, but that in no way diminishes the exercise.

Your self is a product of imagination, so there is no need to get at the actual thoughts. The point here is to simply experience the event from the garment of thought.

Put the thought version aside, and retell the same event from the perspective of the words that were spoken. Just record (remember or invent) what was said, and leave off any reference to thought. For example, do write: "You are the most greedy SOB I have ever met." Don't write: "I was so frustrated that I just wanted to lash out at him, to hurt him the way he had hurt me. I was boiling with rage at the thought he would stay with me, and boiling with terror at the thought he would not. I said, 'You are the most greedy SOB I have ever met.'"

Put the word version aside and retell the story again from the point of view of the third garment, deeds. In this retelling, focus on action. What did you do? What did the other(s) do in response to what you did? How did you react physically to their response? The deeds here need not be overt. You may have reacted with raised blood pressure and a pain in the pit of your stomach. Write that. Just avoid all thoughts and words in this version of the story.

When you have written each version from its own perspective go back and reread them. Now rewrite the story as a conversation among the three garments. Imagine they are each self-aware perspectives who meet to try and figure out what happened. Don't be afraid to have the garments in conflict with one another. Our thoughts, words, and deeds are often at odds, so use this exercise to explore that.

CHAPTER FOUR

WRITING TO
OPEN THE SOUL

One of the best ways to understand the dimension of soul is to go back to the level of mind and compare the two. This is decidedly the mind's preference even though it will come out on the losing end of the comparison. Compare and contrast is what the mind does. Its world is one of either/or, while the dimension of soul is about both/and.

While it is admittedly a stretch from a philosophical point of view, I find the work of Martin Buber (1878–1965), specifically his articulation of the two primary word pairs *I-It* and *I-Thou*, to be the best way to explain the dimension of soul.

Sometime during 1923, Buber experienced an inward clarity "so manifestly suprapersonal in its nature that I at once knew I had to bear witness to it."[1] This bearing witness resulted in the small classic he titled *Ich und Du* (*I and Thou*). The quality of the I in each relationship depends on whether it is relating to an It or a Thou. When relating to an It, the I is the narrow mind of self intent on using the It as an object to further the mind's own ends. When relating to a Thou, another in every way equal in value to the I, the I is the I of soul, the I that knows all beings to be part of the singular Being I call God.

The mind dimension of the spiral is the dimension of I-It. The soul dimension is the dimension of I-Thou. Whenever you step outside the mind's narrow notion of self and experience the I of I-Thou you are in the dimension of soul. Where Buber focuses on the singularity of any given relationship, the Vietnamese Zen master Thich Nhat Hanh applies the same notion to the entirety of the world. He calls this *inter-being*.

Reality does not permit separate things; everything is linked to everything else. Everything "inter-is." When you look at the paper on which this book is written you should be able to see a cloud, for without clouds there is no rain, and without rain there are no trees, and without trees there is no paper. And if you look more closely you should be able to the see the sun as well, and the logger who harvested the tree, and the mill worker who turned it into pulp and the pulp into paper. If you look closer still you will see the logger's parents, and their parents, and every generation of life-form that ever was, for all the was is necessary for the birth of all that is. "To be is to inter-be. You cannot just be by yourself alone. You have to inter-be with every other thing. This sheet of paper is, because everything else is."[2]

The soul dimension is that state of awareness where you, the I of soul, know everything is part of a singular reality of inter-being and see all others as Thous, as precious to life as you are.

Every person born into this world represents something new, something that never existed before, something original and unique. "It is the duty of every person in Israel to know and consider that he is unique in the world in his particular character and that there has never been anyone like him in the world, for if there had been someone like him, there would have been no need for him to be in the world. Every single man is a new thing in the world, and is called upon to fulfill his particularity in this world...." Every man's foremost task is the actualization of his unique, unprecedented and never-recurring potentialities, and not the repetition of something that another, and be it even the greatest, has already achieved.[3]

In the I-It dimension of mind the I is unique and precious, but the It (the "other," be it animal, vegetable, mineral, or human) is not. The It is there to be of service to the I. In the dimension of soul, the I is no less unique and precious, but now knows all others as equally unique and precious as well. That is what a Thou is: an I in and of itself in relation to you. You are I to yourself and Thou to the other, and the other is I to itself and Thou to you. And you know this intimately. Hence, there is no exploitation of the other as It, only a mutual engagement with the other as Thou. Given the demands of English grammar this sounds more complicated than it is, but if you sit with this for a moment it will become clear to you.

Lung

Imagine your lungs could speak. I know it may sound silly, but part of writing to open the soul is to inspire body, heart, and mind to look beyond their limits to see the greater picture, the view from inter-being. So for the sake of this exercise, your lungs can speak. Now interview them. Ask them, and of course provide the answers to, the following questions:

1. There is no question, Lungs, that you are essential to the well-being of this body, but can you do your job alone? What other aspects of the body are essential to your functioning the way you are central to theirs?
2. What about outside the body? I realize that you are linked to oxygen, but neither you nor any other aspect of the body produces oxygen. Where does

this come from, and because you can't function
without it are these oxygen producers not also part
of you?

3. Let's talk more about these oxygen producers.
   What do they rely upon? Earth, sun, rain, what?
   And if they rely on these can you say that these
   larger systems are part of you?

4. Is there any limit to this sense of inter-being? And if
   not, is it true in a literal way that you are the world?
   Maybe even the universe?

What the Self knows, and what the self has to hear, is the
message of inter-being, and when it does you experience the
quality of amazement, wonder. The soul is in a state of constant
amazement, and when self slips into soul, that amazement is
shared. When does this happen? When an I meets a Thou, when
your I meets another not as an It, an object to be used to achieve
your own ends, but as a unique expression of Life (or God) no
different than your Self.

Listen to Buber on his experience looking into the eyes of a
cat:

> An animal's eyes have the power to speak a great lan-
> guage. Independently, without needing co-operation of
> sounds and gestures, most forcibly when they rely wholly
> on their glance, the eyes express the mystery.... Sometimes
> I look into a cat's eyes ... there enters the glance ... a quality
> of amazement and of inquiry.... [4]

There is something transformative when meeting the gaze of
another, all the more so when that other isn't human. If you have
an animal in your life, if you are a guardian to a dog, cat, horse,
or bird, you may know what Buber is talking about. Something
magical happens when you peer into the eyes of your beloved

animal companion. (Notice my avoidance of the term "pet." A pet is an It to an owner's I. Buber is talking about an animal as a Thou, and from that perspective the term "pet" cannot apply.)

I'm not talking about some romanticized encounter where you imagine the feelings of your friend and reciprocate in kind. I am talking about the actual glance itself. There is a consciousness there that is meeting you, and it is in that meeting of minds— what Rilke calls "two solitudes saluting one another"—that one discovers the I-Thou relationship, the glance that passes from soul to soul. When this happens the experience of amazement is undeniable, but there is more.

This glance, Buber says, is marked not only by its quality of amazement, but also by a sense of inquiry. The I of I-It can be shocked, surprised, and horrified, but not truly curious. Of course, the I of I-It can be inquisitive, but only as long as the object of its inquiry seems to possess something of value that the I of I-It can use. This is at best an objectifying relationship, at worst an exploitative one. It is by no means the simple curiosity of an I on the verge of meeting a Thou that Buber values.

Amazing Gazing

I'm going to focus this prompt on a dog, but you should feel free to substitute any animal with which you feel comfortable.

Get down on the floor with your dog. Don't force her to face you, but simply invite her attention. Talk to her and notice what you experience when she looks into your eyes. Don't imagine what she is thinking. Don't put words in her mouth. Just notice what you are experiencing whenever you gaze into one another's eyes.

Write down your side of this encounter. Note the wonder you may feel communing with another species. Note the curiosity that arises within you. Don't put content to it; simply describe the experience. Putting

words to it takes you out of the experience. Just write
the almost ineffable luminosity that arises when you and
your dog meet.

Buber equates this kind of curiosity to what Moses experienced
at the burning bush.

> Moses was shepherding the sheep of his father-in-law
> Jethro, the priest of Midian.... [H]e looked and saw a bush
> ablaze but not consumed. Moses said, "I must leave this
> path and inquire into this great sight...." When God saw
> that he had turned aside to see, God called to him out
> of the bush, "Moses, Moses!" And Moses replied, "Here
> I am." Then God said, "Come no closer! Remove your
> sandals from your feet, for the place on which you stand
> is holy ground." (Exodus 3:1–5; my translation)

Moses had passed this way many times in his decades of
shepherding his father-in-law's sheep, yet this time something
was different, and a difference he had to investigate. Moses left
the path he had trodden for years, and only when he does so
does God speak to him. The trigger was Moses turning, and
the result was God calling out his name twice. Why twice? The
first time to catch the I of I-It; the second time to affirm the I
of I-Thou.

The call of God and the response of Moses are immediate
and profound. The Thou calls to Moses by name—no one else
can be intended—and the named responds with "Here *I* am!"
This is the I of soul, the I of I-Thou. And the first thing this I
must do is remove its sandals.

Sandals here refer to anything that separates you from the
holy ground on which you stand at this very moment. According
to Buber, this is what God says to each of us: take off your

sandals, "put off the habitual which encloses your foot and you will recognize that the place on which you happen to be standing at this moment is holy ground."[5] You are standing on holy ground right now. Wherever you are at this very moment is holy ground. The problem is that the self (the I of I-It) doesn't know it; only the Self (the I of I-Thou) can know it. To realize the holiness of this place you must remove your sandals, free yourself from the habitual, the conditioning that defines you. This is the challenge of all spirituality. Here is how you might experience it when writing as a spiritual practice.

Shoeless Moe, Part 1: Identifying Your Sandals

What are the sandals that are keeping you from standing barefoot on holy ground? Clearly we aren't talking about physical sandals. We are talking about conceptual sandals: those thoughts and systems of belief that keep you in your story and prevent you from experiencing the world without it. Your stories are your sandals. List them. Write down the ideas that shape your self. Some of these you have identified earlier, but list them again here: race, gender, religion, political affiliation, class, whatever defines you. Be specific and detailed in your writing. Don't simply write, Democrat, Republican, or Independent, write about the kind of Democrat, Republican, or Independent you are. Spell out your beliefs in each category, writing at least one or two paragraphs for each.

We will return to your "sandals" in a moment, but first we have to see what this call from God is all about. The key is found earlier in the Bible when God calls to Abram (soon to be called Abraham) in the book of Genesis: "Now God said to Abram, 'Lech lecha from your country and your kin and your parents' home and travel to the land that I will show you ... so that you will be a blessing ... so that through you all the families of the earth shall be blessed'" (Genesis 12:1–3). *Lech lecha* means walk (*lech*) toward your Self (*lecha*). In order to turn the spiral from self to Self, from mind to soul, you have to leave behind all the conditioning, all the sandals, you have inherited. Everything must go if you are to go.

Where are you going? God doesn't say! You are to leave all you know to go to a place you have never been and that God will show you only when you arrive there. Now there is a journey of radical trust.

Why are you going? To be a blessing to all the families of earth. *All* the families of earth: vegetable and mineral, animal and human. This isn't the journey of self or the I of I-It. There is no self-serving quality to this journey. Even though God says Abram's family will become numerous and famous, their numbers and their fame are not for themselves at all but in order to spread the blessing Abram is called to bring.

This is the journey you must make, and writing as a spiritual practice can be a way to make it. You have identified your sandals, the conditioning of nation, kin, parents, and so forth. Now it is time to remove them.

Shoeless Moe, Part 2: *Lech Lecha*

The way to remove your sandals is to do what God called Abram to do: journey inward. Take the list of those things that keep you from standing barefoot on the ground, naked in the moment; the ideas that prevent you from seeing the world as soul sees it: holy, wondrous, and amazing. Read these things carefully, and as you do notice a greater you observing the reading you. As you read each one, notice whether the greater you is conditioned by these things or is simply aware of the lesser you that is so conditioned. Is the soul male or female? Conservative or liberal? Is the observing you, the soul, any of the things it observes? Write what the soul observes, and observe that the soul itself cannot be observed.

As you practice this exercise, you are traveling to the land of promise, the fourth turning of the spiral, the place of authentic meeting: the dimension of awareness called soul.

The gift of arriving at soul, however, isn't personal. That is to say, there is no benefit to the I of I-It to turn toward and release the I of I-Thou. The benefit is not to the I at all, but to the Thou. Abraham isn't made great for his own sake, but in order to be a blessing to others. It isn't that Abraham is blessed, but that he becomes a vehicle for blessing others, all others. No one and nothing is left out of the blessing that happens when you turn the spiral and open to the dimension of Self and soul.

Why, then, would the I of I-It turn toward and release the I of I-Thou? There are two answers to this question. First, the self, the I of I-It, is intrinsically anxious. It sees the world as "other," and imagines itself to be alone. It suffers from a deep and unshakable alienation that it seeks to overcome through accumulating as many Its as possible. These Its may be money, power, influence, objects, degrees, awards, accolades, children ... the list is almost endless. The problem is that there is nothing "out there" that will satisfy the inward angst of the self, the I of I-It. So it is from sheer desperation that the I of I-It dares to turn toward the I of I-Thou.

The second answer builds on the first. While the self may become so desperate that it risks opening to the Self, the opening itself, the turning itself, is not a matter of egoic will but non-egoic grace. That is to say, while you can prime the pump of Self and prepare the self to drink from its living waters, you cannot force the waters to flow or the Self to appear. All you can do is turn aside and see; you cannot make God appear in the bush. The prompts that follow will not, then, guarantee you a turning from self to Self. What they will do is help prime the pump.

Against the Pathetic Fallacy

The pathetic fallacy refers to our tendency to ascribe human motives and human consciousness to nature. You are guilty of the pathetic fallacy when you imagine that a tornado spared your house, or that your dog was after vengeance when he chewed your best pair of shoes. The problem with the pathetic fallacy is that it is really an extension of ego, a kind of transference in which we imagine that the world behaves as we do, operating from the confines of a linguistically shaped, self-conscious selfhood.

This is not to say that there is no nonhuman consciousness in the world, just that whatever that consciousness is, it is inevitably going to be different from our own. We cannot meet this consciousness as long as we demand that it operate according to our rules. We must meet it, instead, without preconceptions, and without the need to lock it into some system of understanding. We cannot understand, but we *can* experience.

One way to do this is to seek out a consciousness we know for certain is not human—that is to say, an animal consciousness. This you did in the exercise called Amazing Gazing. Here you will go a bit farther. Practice gazing on other consciousnesses: plants, trees, bugs, rocks.

For example, pick up a rock and hold it in the palm of your hand. Roll it around to get a feel for the rock. Turn it slowly and gaze on every part of its surface. Don't anthropomorphize the rock, simply allow yourself to be amazed by it. Write down your experience. Did the rock gaze back?

Blackout Poems

The Blackout Poem was developed by writer Austin Kleon out of a long history of deformational writing. Deformational writing involves taking an existing piece of writing and altering it (through redaction, through rearrangement, through overwriting, and other methods) so that it is transformed into something new. In Kleon's work, a poem is constructed out of newspaper and magazine articles using redaction. One simply takes a black Sharpie, or similar marker, and colors over the existing text of the article, leaving only the words, phrases, and sentences that one wants, until a poem emerges out of the original piece.

What makes this technique particularly useful to writing as a spiritual practice is that in "blacking out" these articles, one is encouraged to engage with writing in a way that is quite different from the usual approach. Too often we imagine that, in some way or other, writing is a form self-expression. In a Blackout Poem, however, our "self" is blocked. We cannot express what is not already available to us in the text we are working with. If a word or an image or a phrase is not already there, written by the original author, we cannot use it. In fact, we cannot *express* anything at all, because the process of creating the Blackout Poem is not expressive. It is, instead, transformative. Literally. We transform the original text into something new; we also transform our own writing, discovering in the source text images and ideas that we may never have found in ourselves.

This is the real power of the Blackout Poem. It is an act of delayed collaboration between disparate authors. And in this sense it is a perfect manifestation of the "I-Thou" glance. We are, in writing Blackout Poetry, cultivating a kind of living attention, an awareness that cannot be separated from the object it observes but instead takes full part in the continuing life of that object, shaping and being shaped in its turn.

The Exquisite Corpse

The Exquisite Corpse, or *Cadavre Exquis*, is a collaborative artistic game developed by the surrealists in the early twentieth century (accounts vary, but it seems certain the game was invented between 1918 and 1925). The game can be played with any number of players and there are, in fact, multiple versions—some for writing, others for drawing and painting. The version that interests us here, however, is focused specifically on sentence construction, and it takes advantage of the relatively rigid set of syntactical rules governing word order in English (or, in the game's original version, French).

English sentences, at their most simplified, tend to follow a relatively predictable structure: subject, verb, object; or noun, verb, noun. We can complicate this somewhat by adding adjectives, but even then the order of the words remains constant because, in English, adjectives precede the nouns that they describe. The Exquisite Corpse capitalizes on this predictability, crafting sentences that follow the order: adjective, noun, verb, adjective, noun. However, what makes the Exquisite Corpse rather fun is that it adds an element of chance to writing by randomizing the actual words that fill these syntactical positions.

Here's how to play:

1. Gather a group of friends, three paper bags (or other containers), and a stack of note cards.
2. Designate each bag by type of word: adjective, noun, or verb.

3. Have each group member write a single adjective, noun, or verb on a note card, fold the card so that the word is invisible, and place the folded card in the appropriate bag.
4. Repeat as many times as you like.
5. Finally, pull the cards from the containers in order: adjective, noun, verb, adjective, noun.
6. Read the sentences you have created.

Of course, you may be wondering why you should bother. In answer, I can only turn to André Breton, the founder of surrealism, who had this to say about the sentences created by the game: "The Exquisite Corpse will resemble you." What Breton may have meant by this is utterly opaque, and yet I will testify that there is a strange resonance, a magic, to many of the sentences created by the game. They do, somehow, plumb the depths of our collective unconscious, revealing shared insights that cannot be fully accounted for. What is more, they offer us a way out of the limitations of expression created by writing alone, as well as out of the limitations of sensibility created by the rational mind.

As such, they represent a unique tool for writing to open the soul. By circumventing the control exerted by our rational selves, the Exquisite Corpse sentences explode the idea of writing as a form self-expression and replace it with the idea that writing is a form of intimate encounter with the other: in fact, with multiple others. Moreover, by substituting random chance for artistic control, these sentences—the ones that work—confront us with the possibility that we ourselves are never really in control of the creative act. We take part in it, we shape it, but it is not our own. It is, instead, a collaboration with a consciousness beyond our limited understanding. Call it collective consciousness or God; either way, the game puts us into direct contact with the creative will of the universe, and so helps us turn the spiral of the five worlds outward from the I-It of the mind to the I-Thou of the soul.

We can, of course, take the prompt a step further, engaging as writers with the sentences created by this random conjunction of wills. How? By using the sentences that resonate with us as further prompts for writing. As you play, keep an ear open and an eye out for the sentences that stick. Make a list of them and, when you have enough, ask each member of your group to select one and write for ten to fifteen minutes with that sentence as a goad—you might use it as a title or an opening line, or simply write in response to it, exploring whatever ideas it brings to you. Share those writings with your group. In this way too you can meet the "glance" of the other, experiencing the writing of your friends not as something separate from your creative process, but as something deeply linked with that process, sharing in the same divine spark, a spark reflected in infinite variation as it passes through the prism of selfhood.

The Giving Tree Revisited

Shel Silverstein's The Giving Tree is a brutal, horrifying, and beautiful expression of I-It, and because it is so well done, it can provide us with a wonderful writing exercise to get in touch with I-Thou. On the off chance that you are not familiar with the book, here is the story in brief:

The book tells the story of a little boy and an apple tree. The boy uses the tree to make himself happy. He eats of its fruit, swings from its branches, and takes shade beneath its leaves. The tree is only too happy to make the boy happy. After all, we are told, the tree loves the boy.

As the boy grows older his demands on the tree become more aggressive. He cuts down its branches to build a house, and chops down the trunk from which to carve a canoe. At the end of both their lives the boy, now an old man, sits on the tree, now a mere stump, and finds comfort.

While readers can debate Shel Silverstein's intent when writing *The Giving Tree*—is this a parable of exploitation or martyrdom or both?—for our purposes the story is a prompt, a springboard for exploring the dimension of soul. For the purposes of this exercise you should have a copy of *The Giving Tree* on hand, but if you don't you can still proceed.

Part 1: Imagine you are the boy in *The Giving Tree*. You've been using this tree to satisfy your desires for your entire life, a life that is now coming to a close. The tree is nothing but a stump, but you find comfort in sitting on it. You are the I and the tree is the It. Explain to the tree why you did what you did, and what you are feeling now.

Part 2: Imagine you are the tree in *The Giving Tree*. Explain to the boy what is was like to be his It. You kept saying that being used made you happy? In what way?

Part 3: Imagine you are the old man in *The Giving Tree*, but this time speak from the perspective of I-Thou. The tree isn't an It but a Thou, a being with whom you have a mutual relationship. Tell the tree how you feel about how you have lived with regard to her.

Part 4: Go outside and sit with a real tree. Do as Buber did and analyze the tree from the I-It perspective. Note its species and kind. See how it interacts with earth, wind, sun, and sky. Be as moved as you wish by the tree, but maintain the objective stance of I-It. And then drop it.

Part 5: Engage with the tree as Thou, as a unique being who "inter-is" with you. Without forgetting anything you know, know something more: know the tree to be your partner in the I-Thou reality that is the soul dimension of our spiral. Converse with the tree through writing. Speak to the tree as to a dear friend and beloved, and discover her to be just that.

Glimpsing the Bush

Moses was walking the same trails he had walked for decades when he glimpsed the bush and turned aside to see it up close. Notice the Bible doesn't say the bush suddenly started burning when Moses walked by. There is no reason to believe the burning bush was a new event; it could have been burning every time Moses walked his sheep along this path. What was new this time wasn't the burning bush, but Moses noticing it.

Chances are you too have walked the same path for years—physical, psychological, spiritual—and chances are you walked preoccupied with whatever was happening in your life, so preoccupied that you never noticed the burning bushes all around you. This exercise is designed to change that.

Go for a walk in your neighborhood or along streets you have walked many times before. Take a notebook and pen with you. As you walk along, look for the new and unusual, and jot down what you see in your notebook. Perhaps it is a dog prancing around in a fountain or park or a couple arguing or being loving toward one another. I doubt you will find a bush or anything else on fire while not being consumed, but you will find all kinds of life unfolding in ways you would normally pass by without notice. In this exercise, notice everything.

As life comes into view note as well how the events you are noticing affect your thoughts and feelings. What comes up for you as you take a closer look at the life unfolding all around you?

When you come home from this walk take one or two of these glimpses and your responses to them and explore them more fully. Answer the question: "Why did I respond this way?" Don't do too much self-analysis here, just write what first comes to you. In a day or two review what you have written and see what you can learn from it.

Done well, the writing during the walk and just after is a conduit for Self to speak to self. The rereading a day or two later is the self hearing what is spoken.

A Day in the Wilderness

In Genesis we are challenged to free ourselves from our external conditioning: the norms of nation, tribe, and family that define us. In Exodus we are challenged to remove our sandals, our internal habits of body, heart, and mind that condition us no less than those imposed from without. When we remove our habits we no longer know how to live; we lack an agenda, a plan, and all premeditation. We have entered the wilderness, and we can only respond to what is as it appears to us in the moment.

Most of us choose to avoid the wilderness, and to remain behind the veil of habit. We know how to respond to the next moment by repeating how we responded in the last moment. We live in the past as a defense against the rawness of the present. This is where the self feels most comfortable. Life is an It, an object to be manipulated, and we learn how to manipulate it over time through trial and error. Eventually, we become proficient at this by winnowing out behaviors that do not yield desired results and making habitual those behaviors that do yield desired results.

Of course, what those results may be have nothing to do with what is best for you and your life and the lives of those you love. There are plenty of bad habits to which you can become enslaved, but it is still true that at least in the beginning this bad habit provided you with some desired result.

In this exercise you will live a day in the wilderness, a day without habits. OK, this is probably impossible in any absolute sense, so just do your best.

Look at your calendar and pick a day that you can devote to living wildly. This may be a day when you don't have to go to work or school, or you may be bold and try to live wildly in the midst of your everyday obligations. However you decide to do this, pick a day and live it as a pure experiment.

Set your intention to do whatever life calls you to do. Perhaps someone walks up to you and asks for directions—walk him to where he is going. Or you notice trash on the sidewalk—pick it up. In short, make yourself of service to life free from your own agenda. Live the day as if you were standing on holy ground, and everything that comes to you to do comes as a commandment from God. Just do it.

Keep a pad and pen with you throughout the day and take note of what you do and how it affects you.

Most people who do this exercise have reported that it lifts them outside the self and fills them with compassion that is the hallmark of the Self.

CHAPTER FIVE

WRITING TO
OPEN THE SPIRIT

If the self of the dimension of mind is the I of Buber's I-It, and the Self of the dimension of soul is the I of Buber's I-Thou, we might extend Buber's thinking to the realm of the spirit where all Its and Thous are revealed to be pure subjectivity: the I-I, if you like.

Buber himself doesn't speak this way. His passion is for dialogue, especially dialogue between I and Thou. Dialogue needs partners, but in the dimension of spirit there is no other, there are no partners. There is only the One without second, only the I Am.

To help clarify the reality of the spirit, allow me to review what we have learned thus far. Let's turn back to the analogy of ocean and wave briefly mentioned in the introduction. In that metaphor the Self or soul was the ocean and the self or mind was the wave. Each wave is unique and non-repeatable, and yet each wave is an expression of the singular ocean. At its least aware, the self of mind, the I of I-It, sees itself as wave, but not as ocean. It imagines that it is other than the world in which it resides. This otherness produces a sense of alienation, and this alienation gives rise to an underlying fear: the fear of death, the fear of crashing against the shore. This fear, in humans, not waves, often erupts as anger resulting in acts of violence. The I of mind, the I of I-It, is alone and desperate to avoid its own demise. "I" wants to live forever and invents many different stories that seek to ally its fears of death.

The I of I-Thou, the I of soul, is the ocean, and because all waves are extensions of the ocean, the I of soul, the Self, knows itself to be the waves as well. Understanding this is essential to understanding the turnings from mind to soul and soul to spirit. A common mistake is to imagine that at the level of Self there is no more self, or at the level of ocean there are no more waves. This is not the case at all. The person awake in the soul dimension doesn't lose her mind, she simply ceases to see her mind in isolation from all other minds. As you turn through the spiral from body to heart to mind to soul, nothing is lost. You still have a body, you still have feelings, you still have thoughts. What changes is that you are no longer driven by any of these things because you no longer cling to any of them.

Resting in Soul

This exercise is easiest to do if you can touch-type, that is, type without needing to look at the keys of the keyboard. If you can touch-type, use a computer and keyboard for this exercise. If you can't touch-type, you can try writing with your eyes closed on a sheet of paper, or simply use your eyes and do your best not to be distracted by what you see with your eyes.

With your fingers on the keyboard or your pen ready to write, use your soul's eye to notice, and your fingers to write down, all of the physical sensations, feelings, and thoughts that arise in the mind. These will change quickly and you should try and jot them down as fast as you can. Don't worry about spelling, and don't use more than a few words to note what you are observing: right foot itching, grumbling stomach, frustration, anxious about work, and so on.

Practice this way for five minutes or so, and then read your list. If you managed to capture the doings of body, heart, and mind you can't help but be amazed at all the waves they are making.

All these sensations, feelings, and thoughts are yours: they are happening in your body, heart, and mind, but none of them are you from the perspective of soul. You have them, but they don't have you. So it is incorrect to imagine that body, heart, and mind disappear in the dimension of soul. What is correct is to realize that you are not enslaved to the doings of body, heart, and mind.

This is not the first time I've asked you to engage in this kind of realization, but it bears repeating, especially as we seek to glimpse the dimension of spirit. So, where the I of body is driven by pleasure and pain, the I of heart is driven by love and fear, and the I of mind is driven by us and them and the alienation and conflict "us and them" creates, the I of soul is driven by none of these.

What "drives" the I of soul? Its sense of harmony and balance, and a radical acceptance that allows what is to be what is, knowing full well it will become something else momentarily. Because the I of soul sees everything as a manifestation of the One, it knows itself to be *a part of* rather than *apart from* the whole of reality. And because it knows itself as both the wave and the ocean it sees unity *through* diversity, honoring the uniqueness of each Thou without imagining itself to be separated from any Thou.

The I of soul knows pleasure and pain, love and fear, uniqueness and unity, and does so without the mind's insistence on otherness. The I of soul is awake to, and aware of, all that arises in body, heart, and mind, but it just no longer has the need to forcefully change what arises. Unlike the I of mind that seeks to impose its will on the world "out there," the I of soul works with what arises to bring about peace and harmony without the illusion that waves and ocean are two separate things. There is no "us and them" in the dimension of soul, only us.

The I of I-I is something greater still. If the I of mind is the wave, and the I of soul is the ocean that waves, the I of spirit is wetness itself. While the ocean is the wave and the wave is the ocean, they differ in degree. No one would mistake any given wave for the entirety of the ocean that waves it. The ocean is greater than its waves, and each wave or even the sum of all waves is still less than the ocean as a whole. Not so with wetness. No wave is wetter than any other, and no wave is less wet than the ocean, and the ocean is not wetter than its waves. Wetness is present in all as all equally.

Nothing of substance can be said of the I-I. It cannot be observed, for there is no other to observe it. As such, it cannot be written about, or talked about, or conceptualized in any way. Metaphor and analogy is the best I can do, and even these fall far short of the reality of I-I itself. As Heisenberg pointed out, to the dismay of science, to observe a thing is to alter that thing. So it is with the dimension of spirit. To speak of the I-I is to instantly make it an object, and as soon as we have done that it is no longer the eternal subject, the I Am. So let's not waste time speculating on what is beyond words and experiment with writing that points us beyond words.

BEYOND WORDS

The following exercises are unlike any we have done thus far. They may appear to be nonsense to you, and if they do—congratulations! You're right; they are. Nonsense is the best way to play with the I-I of spirit. These exercises are a form of play for play's sake. There is no point to them outside of them. You won't achieve some enlightened state by doing them. They are meant to point to something that has no place and hence toward which you cannot point. We have entered the realm of paradox, an absurdist realm where Kafka and Nasrudin reign.

A novelist and short-story writer, Franz Kafka (1883–1924) was a master of the absurd, what has come to be called the

Kafkaesque. His tales bring us into a world where reason fails us, and the nonrational points the way. But toward what we cannot say. Listen to Kafka as he attempts to speak what can't be spoken in his story titled "The Departure."

> I ordered my horse to be brought from the stables. The servant did not understand my orders. So I went to the stables myself, saddled my horse, and mounted. In the distance I heard the sound of a trumpet, and I asked the servant what it meant. He knew nothing and had heard nothing. At the gate he stopped me and asked: "Where is the master going?" "I don't know," I said, "just out of here, just out of here. Out of here, nothing else, it's the only way I can reach my goal." "So you know your goal?" he asked. "Yes," I replied, "I've just told you. Out of here—that's my goal."[1]

There's a certain resonance in Kafka's tale with the biblical story of Abraham leaving his father's house, and with the story of Moses and the Israelites fleeing Egypt for forty years in the wilderness. Yet, there is an important difference as well. In those stories, the departure has a destination, the journey has a goal: the Promised Land. Kafka's journey has no goal. In fact, it is inappropriate even to speak of a journey in regard to Kafka. Here, the only goal is departure itself, the grand exit: "out of here."

It may be tempting to read this phrase, "out of here," as an allegory for death. And, in a sense, it is. But I do not believe that Kafka is talking about literal death. He may, rather, be talking about the death of self, the death of the I of mind that imagines itself as existing as a singular entity at a particular place and time. When Kafka says "out of here," he is suggesting that we abandon our sense of here-ness. He wants us to go beyond location, duration, and identity, beyond the perspective that says: "I am I because I am here."

Why? Because we are trapped within that perspective, trapped within the self, and perhaps also trapped within a set of power relations pursuant to selfhood, hierarchies of master to servant, relationships of I to It.

Dying to the self, we absent ourselves from the smallness of self, the narrow field of single-point perspective, and approach our own vanishing point, the infinite horizon of spirit. But, again, "approaching" is the wrong word. As is "horizon." We don't go anywhere. There is no *where* to go. In fact, you might even say that nowhere is precisely where we are headed. And when we get there, we won't be there, because there's nowhere to be.

If this sounds confusing, good: it should. Language doesn't function in the no-where dimension of spirit. Language is too bound up with the dimension of mind. It is only in language that we conceive of this thing or that thing, this place or that place. Language is all about particulars; as Shakespeare put it in *A Midsummer Night's Dream*, language gives "to airy nothing a local habitation and a name."

It's interesting to note, in this regard, that language doesn't function well in Kafka's story either. Throughout, servant and master speak at cross-purposes, misunderstanding each other. Something similar, but more telling, happens in another of Kafka's stories, "On Parables":

> Many complain that the words of the wise are always merely parables and of no use in daily life, which is the only life we have. When the sage says: "Go over," he does not mean that we should cross over to some actual place, which we could do anyhow if the labor were worth it; he means some fabulous yonder, something unknown to us, something too that he cannot designate more precisely, and therefore cannot help us here in the very least. All these parables really set out to say merely that the incomprehensible is incomprehensible, and we know that

already. But the cares we have to struggle with every day: that is a different matter.

Concerning this a man once said: Why such reluctance? If you only followed the parables you yourselves would become parables and with that rid yourself of all your daily cares.

Another said: I bet that is also a parable.

The first said: You have won.

The second said: But unfortunately only in parable.

The first said: No, in reality: in parable you have lost.[2]

Here, too, the desire is to move away from here-ness, to "go over" into the placeless perspective of spirit. And once again, language proves an inadequate medium for describing this change in perspective; the best it can do is to craft parables and metaphors that prove, in the end, incomprehensible, useless. But Kafka's story doesn't stop with this observation. In the conversation that takes up the latter half of the story, we are treated to a different take on the potential spiritual value of language. We are told that we might follow the parables, and so ourselves "become parables and thus free of [our] daily cares." But what does this mean? And how do we do it?

Actually, there's nothing to do. Becoming a parable means recognizing that you already are a parable: that is, an illustration, an analogy. You are not yourself; you are an illustration of Self, your "I" is an analogue to the infinite I of the universe, the infinite I of God. Returning to our earlier metaphor of ocean and wave, we might say that you are neither wave nor ocean; rather, you are the water itself, slipping between form and formlessness. Viewing life from this perspective, our daily cares drop away. Indeed, our entire perception of the events of a day— its frustrations, triumphs, tender moments—is altered. Because we see that whatever happens to us is us, happening.

Let me put it another way. A number of years ago a friend of mine was writing a semi-autobiographical novel about a runaway. His main character, Blis, hitchhikes and hobos across America, eventually getting involved with an ecoterrorist group and later sucked into an ill-considered bank robbery. At a certain point in the writing process, my friend hit a snag. The book was getting pretty dark—horrifying things were happening to Blis—and my friend found that writing a chapter, or a scene, was extremely upsetting. He felt, he said, like whatever happened to Blis in the story was happening to him.

This is what happens to most of us when we read a book: we identify with the main character, the "I" of the story. For writers, especially in a first-person narrative, there is a similar danger. The trick is to remember that when you write, and when you read, everything that occurs in the text occurs because of you. It is all animated by your attention and imagination. So, yes, you can identify with the main character, but by the same token you might identify equally with every character, every object, every event in the story. They're all you. Reading Conan Doyle, for example, you might imagine yourself inhabiting the role of Sherlock Holmes, but you are also inhabiting the role of Dr. Watson, Lestrade, Mycroft, and Moriarty, and by the same token you are playing 221b Baker Street; you are playing the Diogenes Club, you are playing Holmes's violin, playing the pipe clenched in his teeth.

In the movie *The Matrix*, a key step on Neo's journey to enlightenment is his recognition that the world of the Matrix is an illusion. He begins to understand this when a young boy, dressed tellingly in a Buddhist-style robe and sporting a shaven head, teaches him to bend a spoon, saying: "Do not try to bend the spoon. That is impossible. Only try to realize the truth: there is no spoon." This same realization, applied to the self rather than a spoon, is what I am referring to when I talk about "becoming parables."

And language, paradoxically, can help us to this realization. How? By confronting us with paradox, by confronting us, as

Kafka's parable does, with the inadequacy of perspectives that comprehend life via the process of differentiation. This is what happens to the clever man at the end of Kafka's story, who insists on the distinction between parable and reality. He wins, in the everyday dimension of mind, because he insists on distinguishing the literal from the figurative, "reality" from "parable." But he loses in the dimension of spirit because he fails to recognize that the real as we know it—the experience of the senses translated through the apprehensions of the self-conscious mind—is itself a linguistic construct; it is figurative: an analogy, or perhaps a metonymy, for the ineffable reality that is God.

Playing with Paradox, Part 1: Colorless Green Ideas

Generally speaking, we think of a paradox as a statement or series of statements leading to a contradiction that defies logic or intuition. The statement, "This statement is false," is one example, for, if the statement is false, then it must be true, in which case it is false, and so on. Paradoxes challenge our rational model of the universe, revealing that we do not know, or cannot know, reality solely through rational means. As such, they provide a powerful opportunity for writing as a spiritual practice, challenging us to accept the limits of the rational and to take pleasure in the absurd.

There are any number of ways to construct paradoxes, but this prompt will focus on only one: the category mistake. On its own the category mistake is not a paradox. Rather, it is a simple semantic or ontological error in which one ascribes a property to a thing that could not possibly have that property. What is intriguing about the category mistake, though, is that it reveals a fundamental weakness in the structure of language itself. The flaw is this: using category errors, one can write, or speak, a perfectly sensible sentence that nevertheless makes absolutely no sense at all.

Noam Chomsky, in his influential 1957 book *Syntactic Structures*, offers the following example: "Colorless green ideas sleep furiously." What is rather wonderful about this sentence is that it is packed with paradoxical pairings such as "colorless green" and "sleep furiously." At its heart, though, is the category mistake: an idea cannot sleep, nor can it have color. The sentence is perfect, conforming to every rule of grammar and syntax, and yet it is absolutely impossible, semantically speaking. And so we see, for a moment, what language can do when it is unyoked from the tyranny of sense: it *realizes* the impossible in whimsical defiance of the rational.

This is the type of (loosely defined) paradox we will work with in our prompt. The idea is to craft sentences that, like Chomsky's, negate themselves via contradiction and category error. This is, of course, not a prompt that requires any set time frame or that has any particular rules—other than the injunction to write self-contradictory sentences. You may attempt this prompt whenever you feel like it, though it might be helpful to set a goal, say, of writing one a day, or a time frame, of writing for fifteen minutes. I would also suggest keeping all your sentences together, perhaps in a notebook devoted to them, or in a particular file (digital or hardcopy).

Once you have fallen into the practice of writing self-negating sentences, you may take your work further by attempting to extend them and/or combine them, squeezing as many contradictions and category errors into a single sentence as possible, or playing with the possibility of delaying the negation: one could, perhaps, craft clauses that are sensible on their own, but are contradicted by other clauses in the same sentence. How many contradictions can a single sentence hold? Can these sentences become a paragraph? A story? A poem?

You may also experiment with using the sentences as prompts, writing in response to them for a set time (ten or fifteen minutes). Additionally, you might consider using one of the sentences as a title for a poem or story, for example, and then see where it takes you. The point is to play and to explore, allowing the "meaninglessness" of these sentences to push your writing in unexpected directions, to discover where the impossible and nonsensical might lead you, if only you would follow it.

Of course, as with some of our previous prompts, the sentences, stories, poems, or paragraphs that you craft here may or may not result in any kind of special insight. Still, the insight we are seeking here is not in the sentences we create, or in the writing we do in response to those sentences (though it may arise in both places); rather, the insight lies in the practice of creating them. As we work to liberate language from the rational in this way, we work also to free ourselves from the cage of common sense, so we can begin to step outside the narrow boundaries of acceptable meaning and explore the infinite creative potential that is the province of the divine spirit.

Not everyone is comfortable with writing contradictory sentences. It often causes people's stomachs to churn, literally. This is actually a good thing: it means that you are getting "out of here" without the comfort of "going over there." If you found Colorless Green Ideas too upsetting, you may have a better time with the next exercise, Cut-up. If you enjoyed writing paradoxes, you will find Cut-up equally enjoyable.

Playing with Paradox, Part 2: Cut-up

The cut-up technique is exactly what it sounds like. Take a piece of writing, your own or someone else's, Xerox or print it, and then cut it up into sentences, phrases, clauses, images, or other parts. Put the pieces in a bag, shake, and construct a new piece of writing by pulling out one strip of paper at a time. The cut-up can be practiced using a single piece of writing, or—more profitably—using multiple pieces of writing, the more varied the better. In fact, some of the most spectacular results come when you mix pieces of writing from different time periods, or from different cultural registers. For example, you might cut up and recombine a sonnet by Shakespeare with an article from *Vogue* magazine. Or an article from *Wired* with the Declaration of Independence.

Our expectations of language and of writing suggest that the result of Cut-up will be unintelligible. But it won't. Yes, some of it will be incomprehensible, but some of it will make perfect sense, and some of it—perhaps through the sheer bizarreness of the juxtaposition—may actually resonate so powerfully that you are jarred into new perspectives: you have gone "out of here."

The purpose of Cut-up, though, like the purpose of Colorless Green Ideas, lies less in the results than in the process itself. Because what the Cut-up does is create, or reveal, completely improbable harmonies between disparate writings, disparate writers, disparate times, and disparate cultures. In the works created by Cut-up, then, you begin to discern an interconnectedness that transcends every rational boundary, collapsing time, space, and self in a single miraculous collage. Through practicing the Cut-up method, we escape the perspective of "here" and glimpse the perspective of "everywhere."

Which bring us, in a meandering sort of way, to Nasrudin. Nasrudin may once have been a living person, a thirteenth-century Sufi sage who taught through humorous and often paradoxical stories. If that is true, he would be delighted to know that today and for centuries he has become a fictional character starring in hundreds of humorous teaching tales.

As a fictional character in Islamic folklore, Nasrudin is at once fool, trickster, and sage. Stories of Nasrudin are often told as jokes or anecdotes, swapped over dinner or between friends passing in the street: "Hey, have you heard the one about Nasrudin and his wife?" But, like Kafka's stories, Nasrudin tales offer us an opportunity to explore the limits of knowledge, the limits of human perspective and understanding. For example, once, as Nasrudin was walking home from town to his village, he saw some tasty-looking ducks swimming in a pool. Intending to catch and cook the ducks for his dinner, Nasrudin waded into the pool. But the ducks flew away. Unperturbed, Nasrudin took a piece of bread from his pocket, tore it to pieces, and threw the pieces into the water. Then, kneeling, Nasrudin began to drink, cupping the water in his hands. At that moment, a party of townspeople passed along on the road. "Nasrudin!" they shouted; "What are you doing?" "Eating duck soup," he replied.

There are at least two ways to read this story. One reading says that Nasrudin is a fool, and that the story makes a mockery of logical reasoning. After all, there is a logic to Nasrudin's behavior. All the ingredients of duck soup are present, so, from a certain perspective, it is reasonable to conclude that ducks + water + bread = duck soup. Of course, the conclusion is absurd, but that's the point. Life cannot be formulated in this way. It is more than the sum of its parts.

However, there is another way to read this story. In this second reading, Nasrudin is a sage, and his actions, though absurd, are nevertheless precisely correct. He has understood that fantasy and reality are one: that both are products of the imagination, and that he can, through the sheer exuberance of imagination, transform the pond into soup. In this reading of the story, Nasrudin *is* eating duck soup.

Typically, we rebel against this second reading. We want to assert that reality is reality, and that, no matter what, a pond is not a bowl of soup. But that's the point: reality is not reality, it is only a perspective reflecting the frame of mind of the perceiver.

When we read this way we allow the imagination full rein, we turn ever so slightly in the direction of spirit, leaving behind our insistence on the distinction between the real and the fantastic. When we read this way, we are like children, for whom nothing is absurd and all things are possible.

This is the point of the Nasrudin tales. They awaken us to radical faith: not the foolish faith that mistakes story for reality, but the absurd faith that sees reality itself as story. This, too, is the point of writing to open to the dimension of spirit. We have spent quite a bit of time freeing ourselves from our story, and in this way freeing ourselves from the limitations of mind. Now we may return to our stories, not because we believe in them, but because we no longer need to.

My Story, My Sage

Recall a powerful moment from your childhood, a moment when you confronted a great fear or made a great mistake. When told from the perspective of mind, the story is used to build up the self, but when told from the perspective of spirit it can inform the self with an insight the self itself may have missed.

To facilitate this, rewrite the story from the perspective of the Wise Old You. Imagine yourself as a sage, a person whose story no longer owns her. Write of yourself in the third person, and turn your story into a parable.

In Jewish circles a wise elder is called Reb, an honorific title. Think of yourself as Reb Judy, or Reb Mark, and tell a story from your childhood as a parable that unleashes a teaching that helped shape Reb Judy into the person she has now become. Here is an example from a Path & Pen gathering:

The story, used with permission, is from a fifty-something engineer named Jon.

I used to have a terrible fear of dogs. I was certain they would attack me and rip my throat out. I was about eight years old when my parents brought home a puppy. I have no idea why; they knew I was afraid of dogs. Maybe they thought this would get me over it. I started screaming as soon as the puppy came into the house, which scared the dog, who peed on the rug. My dad got angry at both of us, and tossed the dog outside in the backyard and chased me into my room slamming the door as I hid behind my bed. Did I mention I was scared of my dad, too?

Anyway, I hated the dog and wanted him gone. I plotted to get rid of him. A couple of days later I told my parents I wanted to walk the dog in the woods behind our house. They were skeptical at first, but my dad said it would be good for me, so they put the puppy on a leash and sent us out.

I raced ahead and dragged the dog along deep enough into the woods where no one could see us. Then I wrapped the leash around a tree until the dog was pressed against the trunk. I started gathering stones, and planned to stone the dog to death.

It only took a few minutes and I had a pile of rocks ready to throw. I tossed a couple of pebbles at the dog's head just to see what would happen. She ducked and made some odd sound. A whimper I'd say now. I didn't care, I was angry and scared and wanted her dead. I picked up a rock that could have smashed her head wide open if it connected with enough force. I threw it hard, but wide. I missed. I picked up another one and did the same thing: hard and wide.

I was good at throwing balls and these stones were no different, but I kept missing. Then it hit me: I couldn't do it. I didn't want to do it. I just fell to the ground and cried. Eventually I stopped crying, kicked the pile of stones so they mixed in the with ground and untied my dog. My dog. I wasn't afraid or angry. I said I was sorry, and she licked my hand as if to say, "It's OK, I knew you'd come around." We went home. She lived with me for twelve years.

Once you have your story down, retell it as a parable. Here is Jon's:

When Reb Jon was a little boy he had a great fear of dogs. His parents, hoping to help him get over his fear, brought home a dog that they hoped would become his friend. She was a mixed breed, but mostly beagle. She looked like Snoopy from the *Peanuts* cartoons and that is what he called her, but only after he tried to kill her.

His fear spoke to him: "This dog will grow up and grow strong, and she will kill you," it said. And he believed his fear and plotted the dog's death.

Once day Reb Jon took his dog into the woods, tied her to a tree, and planned to stone her to death. As he wrapped her leash around the tree he never saw her face. As he piled the rocks he planned to throw at her head, he never looked at her at all. He tossed tiny pebbles to get himself ready, and she cried. The whimper caught him off guard. He looked at her. He saw her for who she was, another frightened soul just like him. Only she was afraid of him, rather than he of her. The feeling of being feared broke him. "No one should be afraid of me," he whispered. "I want only to love."

He wept as he freed his dog. He wept more as he cuddled her, stroked her head, and told her how sorry he was. He spoke her name over and over and over again, meeting her anew each time. She wasn't his pet, but his friend. He wasn't her owner but her companion. She was as he was: God manifest. It was the beginning of his life of the spirit.

Notice how in Jon's retelling we learn the dog's name and breed. She becomes a Thou, and this is what makes the story a teaching tale, a parable.

CHAPTER SIX

TURNING THE SPIRAL FROM BODY TO SPIRIT

RETURNING—BY WAY OF CONCLUSION

There is a tendency in spiritual work to imagine that the self, the ego, the I of I-It is bad. I fear that you may have gotten that impression from this book as well. It is what happens when spiritual turning gets stuck at the point where self turns toward Self, mind turns toward soul. But when you continue the turning through the dimension of spirit you discover that the I-I is all there is, and therefore there is nothing wrong with I-It and nothing special about I-Thou.

Martin Buber himself affirms this when he tells us that it is natural for the I-Thou moment to pass into I-It, and that every I-It encounter can become a moment of I-Thou meeting. So we are not seeking to eliminate any dimension of reality, but to see them all as suffused with spirit.

This is what is taught in the first-century Buddhist text, Prajñāpāramitā Hṛdaya, or *Heart Sutra*. Perhaps the most famous line of this short exposition of the central teachings of Mahayana Buddhism is this: "Form is emptiness, and emptiness is form.

Form is not other than emptiness and emptiness is not other than form."

Form isn't other than emptiness, nor is emptiness other than form. The one flows into the other and back again. The same is true of our five-dimensional spiral: body/heart/mind/soul aren't other than spirit, and spirit isn't other than body/heart/mind/soul. For our purposes the key is to see spirit in all dimensions, and this happens when you open to spirit by opening through each dimension.

So, please, do not imagine you need live without a self, a story, an I in relationship to an It or a Thou. Indeed, you cannot do so. All you can do, all you need do, is see that all of this is spirit. Once this is seen you can enjoy your story without being obsessed with it.

A fine analogy for this is going to a theater and watching a horror movie. The whole point of watching a horror movie is to get scared. If you sit through the film repeating over and over, "This is fake, it is just a film; this is fake, it is just a film" you will not enjoy the experience of being frightened. You will not get into the story of the film at all. So let yourself go, enjoy being frightened, and know that is why you are there.

But when the movie ends and the house lights come up, let the story go. There is no point in walking out of the theater convinced that the monster inside is stalking you outside. It was a movie. In the theater it was real enough; outside the theater it is not real at all.

The same is true of the stories you tell yourself about yourself in order to create that self. They are real enough, and in their context they make sense. But they don't work outside that context, outside the dimension of mind. So what can you do with them from the perspective of spirit? Enjoy them.

The sad fact is, we don't really enjoy the stories we tell. We imagine that they are real, and so we demand continuity and eschew contradiction and paradox. We want our stories to encompass everything and to fit the world into a nice, neat, comprehensible package. This is vanity. Hubris. Worse, it often results in violence.

If your story and my story can't be reconciled, one of our stories must go! And the only way to kill a story is to kill the storyteller, along with everyone who has ever listened to the story. But if we can liberate ourselves from the desire for fixity, the desire to apprehend life, and instead learn to joyfully embrace competing, contradictory, impossible stories, then we are truly free: free to find truth in story without demanding that our stories be true, free to imagine new stories when the old ones no longer serve, and free to entertain the infinite perspectives and possibilities that story provides.

This is what Albert Camus, the existentialist philosopher, meant when he said that "becoming aware of the absurdity of life frees [us] to plunge into it with every excess." Plunging into life is what writing as a spiritual practice is all about. Plunging into life is pure play: living for the sheer joy of living. The prompts that follow here are about plunging in. They are about using writing to unlock the joy of pure play. And so they are also about using writing to unlock the joy of life.

Homophonic "Translation"

I've placed the word translation in quotation marks to make it clear to you that I'm not talking about actual translation. There is no sense in this exercise of knowing how a word in one language makes itself clear in another. On the contrary, I'm asking you to "translate" from languages you don't know at all. My example comes from the French, a poem by Arthur Rimbaud titled "Les Assis."

You may not know any French. In fact, I hope that is the case. If you do read French, find another poem in a language you don't read. Not knowing what the original text says is central to this exercise.

Copy the poem onto a clean sheet of paper, or type it into your computer. Now "translate" the poem based purely on its sound. That is, read the poem aloud to yourself and replace the French words with English homophones: words in English that sound like what you have read in French. Here is an example from a Path & Pen workshop participant:

She began with a line from Rimbaud: *Et comme il savourait surtout les sombres choses.* She was unaware of the meaning of the line. (If you must know, it translates as "And as he especially savored dark things.") What she "heard" was: "It comes, eel savory, sweet tooth, less some hombre choosey." She then polished it up a bit and got this: "The savory eel comes, less its sweet tooth, [lookin'] for some choosey hombre."

When asked to write about her experience with this exercise, she wrote:

> It was silly, and because it was silly I resisted it. I write to make sense, and this was nonsense. But after a few minutes of grumbling I realized that this was not about making sense at all. It was about listening, and noting what I'm hearing, and letting the words tumble about and tumble out without my ego-editor standing at the gate like a bouncer at a nightclub saying, "This word can come in, this word can't." In the end it was very liberating. I have no idea where what I heard came from, but I can tell you it wasn't from me; at least not the me I think I am when I sit down to write.

Exactly the point. You are looking to release creative energies without the ego's editing. This is writing as nonsense; play for the sake of play. Try it and see what happens. On the next page are two verses from Arthur

Rimbaud's poem "Les Assis" to work with. Remember, write what you hear.

Noir de loupes, grêlés, les yeux cerclés de bagues.

Vertes, leurs doigts boulus crispés à leurs fémurs,
Le sinciput plaqué de hargnosités vagues
Come les floraisons lépreuses des vieux murs;

Ils ont greffé dans des amours épileptiques
Leur fantasque ossature aux grands squelettes noirs
De leurs chaises; leurs pieds aux barreaux rachitiques
S'entrelancent pour les matins et pour les soirs!

Sound for sound's sake; words for word's sake; writing to "get out of here," out of body, out of heart, out of mind, out of soul—this is writing as a spiritual practice. But don't imagine it ends with spirit. When we talk about spirit it becomes just another here from which to get out: out of spirit into mind, into heart, into body, and doing so with the realizing that it is all spirit. There is no "out of" or "into" when we step beyond the analogy of wave and ocean and realize the nonduality of wetness. There is no escape from what is, only the awareness that it is all wet. Which brings me to our last exercise in this book.

Turn and Return

This final exercise seeks to integrate the five turnings we have been exploring: body, heart, mind, soul, and spirit. Begin with an observation from the perspective of body. For example, "I am shaking." Repeat the line, adding to the repetition from the perspective of heart:

I am shaking.
I am shaking
With a fear I cannot fathom.

Repeat all three lines, adding a fourth from the perspective of mind:

> I am shaking.
> I am shaking
> With a fear I cannot fathom
> A fear that is a sign of weakness.

Repeat all five lines, adding to the repetition from the perspective of soul:

> I am shaking.
> I am shaking
> With a fear I cannot fathom
> A fear that is a sign of weakness.
> A weakness that lets in hope.

Repeat all six lines, adding to the repetition from the perspective of spirit:

> I am shaking.
> I am shaking
> With a fear I cannot fathom
> A fear that is a sign of weakness.
> A weakness that lets in hope
> That I might collapse into You once more.

This poem is taken from a Path & Pen workshop. It may or may not be a good poem; good and bad are irrelevant here. We are writing to turn the spiral, not to impress someone with our creativity. Once the poem is written you can play with it to see what else it might yield. In this play you may not change the wording of a previous line, but you may change the punctuation, line breaks, capitalization, and so on, thereby allowing your words to take on new form and new meaning. Here is what arose when playing with this poem:

I am shaking. (body)
I am shaking
with a fear I cannot fathom. (heart)
I am shaking with a fear: "I cannot."
Fathom this and the fear will end. (mind)
I am shaking with a fear: "I cannot."
Fathom this and the fear will end,
fathom this and "I" will end. (soul)
I am shaking with a fear: "I cannot."
Fathom this and the fear will end,
fathom this and "I" will end,
fathom this—
but there is no one left
to fathom anything at all. (spirit)

This book has no point. It aims to convince you of nothing. While it shares a point of view, that point of view is secondary to the exercises it offers. You need not agree with anything you have read here. What matters is that you try the exercises, and do so with a willingness to succeed, a willingness to see what you can see through the use of writing.

There are lots of books about writing and many of them have a spiritual spin. I like many of them, and list them in the bibliography. My hope is that this one will make it into the bibliography of the next person who writes about writing as a spiritual practice. This book isn't meant to be the last word on this topic, just another word.

There is no last word, just the next word.

ACKNOWLEDGMENTS

The ideas and exercises expressed in this book are based on a weekend retreat we call Path & Pen: Writing as Spiritual Practice, now in its seventh year. We want to thank all those who have participated in Path & Pen over the years, for helping us test and retest both the theories and the practices offered in this book.

We are also deeply grateful to Emily Wichland, our editor, who took us seriously enough not to let us get away with flabby thinking and loose writing.

NOTES

INTRODUCTION

1. "From *Biographia Literaria*," in *The Norton Anthology of English Literature*, ed. M. H. Abrams (New York: W.W. Norton, 2006), 2:387.

CHAPTER 1

1. Martin Luther King Jr., *I Have a Dream: Writings and Speeches That Changed the World* (New York: HarperOne, 1992), 88.
2. Rainer Maria Rilke, *Letters to a Young Poet* (Miami, Fla.: BN Publishing, 2009), 12.
3. Robert Frost, *The Road Not Taken: A Selection of Robert Frost's Poems* (New York: Holt Paperbacks, 2002), 270.

CHAPTER 3

1. Charles P. Pierce, *The American Way of Idiocy* (New York: Anchor, 2010).

CHAPTER 4

1. Martin Buber, *I and Thou*, trans. Ronald Gregor Smith (New York: Charles Scribner's Sons, 1958), 123.
2. Thich Nhat Hanh, *The Heart of Understanding: Commentaries on the Prajñāpāramitā Heart Sutra* (Berkeley, Calif.: Parallax Press, 2009), 4.
3. Martin Buber, *The Way of Man According to the Teaching of Hasidism* (New York: Citadel Press Books, 2006), 12–13.
4. Buber, *I and Thou*, 94–95.
5. Buber, *The Way of Man*, 45.

CHAPTER 5

1. Franz Kafka, *The Complete Stories*, ed. Nahum N. Glatzer (New York: Schocken Books, 1983), 449.
2. Kafka, *The Complete Stories*, 449.

SUGGESTIONS FOR
FURTHER READING

Alter, Robert. *The Book of Psalms: A Translation with Commentary*. New York: W.W. Norton, 2009.

Atkinson, Robert. *The Gift of Stories: Practical and Spiritual Applications of Autobiography, Life Stories, and Personal Mythmaking*. Westport, Conn.: Bergin & Garvey, 1995.

Baldwin, Christina. *Calling the Circle: The First and Future Culture*. New York: Bantam, 1998.

———. *The Seven Whispers: A Spiritual Practice for Times Like These*. Novato, Calif.: New World Library, 2002.

Bausch, William. *Storytelling: Imagination and Faith*. Mystic, Conn.: Twenty-Third Publications, 1984.

Bennett, Hal Zina. *Writing Spiritual Books*. Maui, Hawaii: Inner Ocean Publishing, 2004.

Buber, Martin. *I and Thou*. Trans. Ronald Gregor Smith. New York: Charles Scribner's Sons, 1958.

———. *I and Thou*. Trans. Walter Kaufmann. New York: Touchstone, 1971.

Cameron, Julia. *The Artist's Way*. New York: Putnam, 1992.

Conner, Janet. *Writing Down Your Soul*. San Francisco: Conari Press, 2008.

Davis, Jeff. *The Journey from the Center to the Page*. New York: Gotham Books, 2004.

DeSalvo, Louise. *Writing as a Way of Healing: How Telling Our Stories Transforms Our Lives*. Boston: Beacon Press, 1999.

Frymer-Kensky, Tikva. *In the Wake of the Goddesses: Women, Culture, and the Biblical Transformation of Pagan Myth*. New York: The Free Press, 1992.

Goldberg, Natalie. *Writing Down the Bones*. Boston: Shambhala, 2005.

―――. *Wild Mind*. New York: Bantam Books, 1990.

Hanh, Thich Nhat. *The Heart of Understanding: Commentaries on the Prajñāpāramitā Heart Sutra*. Berkeley, Calif.: Parallax Press, 2009.

Herman, Deborah. *Spiritual Writing*. Hillsboro, Ore.: Beyond Words Publishing, 2004.

Herring, Laraine. *Writing Begins with the Breath*. Boston: Shambhala, 2007.

Hirshfield, Jane. *Nine Gates: Entering the Mind of Poetry*. New York: Harper Perennial, 1998.

Holberg, Jennifer. *Shouts and Whispers*. Grand Rapids, Mich.: Eerdmans, 2006.

Hughes, Elaine. *Writing from the Inner Self*. New York: HarperCollins, 1991.

Jepson, Jill. *Writing as a Sacred Path*. Berkeley, Calif.: Celestial Arts, 2008.

Kramer, Kenneth Paul. *Martin Buber's I and Thou: Practicing Living Dialogue*. New York: Paulist Press, 2003.

McDowell, Robert. *Poetry as Spiritual Practice*. New York: Free Press, 2008.

Merton, Thomas. *Echoing Silence: On the Vocation of Writing*. Boston: New Seeds, 2007.

Metzger, Donna. *Writing for Your Life: A Guide and Companion to the Inner Worlds*. San Francisco: HarperSanFrancisco, 1992.

Ouaknin, Marc-Alain. *Mysteries of the Alphabet: The Origins of Writing*. New York: Abbeville Press, 1999.

Pearcey, Nancy. *Total Truth: Liberating Christianity from Its Cultural Captivity*. Wheaton, Ill.: Crossway Books, 2004.

Pierce, Charles P. *Idiot America: How Stupidity Became a Virtue in the Land of the Free*. New York: Anchor, 2010.

Pinker, Stephen. *The Language Instinct: How the Mind Creates Language*. New York: William Morrow, 1994.

Rumi, Jalal al-Din. *The Rumi Collection*. Ed. Kabir Helminski. Boston: Shambhala, 2005.

Shapiro, Rami. *The Divine Feminine in Biblical Wisdom Literature: Selections Annotated and Explained*. Woodstock, Vt.: SkyLight Paths, 2005.

————. *Ecclesiastes: Annotated and Explained*. Woodstock, Vt.: SkyLight Paths, 2010.

————. *Ethics of the Sages: Pirke Avot—Annotated and Explained*. Woodstock, Vt.: SkyLight Paths, 2006.

————. *Hasidic Tales: Annotated and Explained*. Woodstock, Vt.: SkyLight Paths, 2004.

————. *The Hebrew Prophets: Annotated and Explained*. Woodstock, Vt.: SkyLight Paths, 2004.

————. *Proverbs: Annotated and Explained*. Woodstock, Vt.: SkyLight Paths, 2011.

————. *Recovery—The Sacred Art: The Twelve Steps as Spiritual Practice*. Woodstock, Vt.: SkyLight Paths, 2009.

————*The Sacred Art of Lovingkindness: Preparing to Practice*. Woodstock, Vt.: SkyLight Paths, 2006.

Sher, Gail. *One Continuous Mistake*. New York: Penguin, 1999.

————. *Writing the Fire*. New York: Bell Tower, 2006.

Silverstein, Shel. *The Giving Tree*. New York: HarperCollins, 2004.

Vecchione, Patrice. *Writing and the Spiritual Life*. New York: Contemporary Books, 2001.

Wheatley, Margaret. *Turning to One Another: Simple Conversations to Restore Hope to the Future*. San Francisco: Berrett-Koehler, 2002.

Wolf, Maryanne. *Proust and the Squid*. New York: Harper Perennial, 2007.

notes

notes

Inspiration

Restoring Life's Missing Pieces
The Spiritual Power of Remembering & Reuniting with People, Places, Things & Self
by Caren Goldman
A powerful and thought-provoking look at reunions of all kinds as roads to remembering and re-membering ourselves.
6 x 9, 208 pp, Quality PB, 978-1-59473-295-9 **$16.99**

How Did I Get to Be 70 When I'm 35 Inside?
Spiritual Surprises of Later Life
by Linda Douty
Encourages you to focus on the inner changes of aging to help you greet your later years as the grand adventure they can be.
6 x 9, 208 pp, Quality PB, 978-1-59473-297-3 **$16.99**

Spiritually Healthy Divorce: Navigating Disruption with Insight & Hope
by Carolyne Call
A spiritual map to help you move through the twists and turns of divorce.
6 x 9, 224 pp, Quality PB, 978-1-59473-288-1 **$16.99**

Who Is My God? 2nd Edition
An Innovative Guide to Finding Your Spiritual Identity
by the Editors at SkyLight Paths
Provides the Spiritual Identity Self-Test™ to uncover the components of your unique spirituality.
6 x 9, 160 pp, Quality PB, 978-1-59473-014-6 **$15.99**

God the What?
What Our Metaphors for God Reveal about Our Beliefs in God
by Carolyn Jane Bohler
Inspires you to consider a wide range of images of God in order to refine how you imagine God.
6 x 9, 192 pp, Quality PB, 978-1-59473-251-5 **$16.99**

Journeys of Simplicity
Traveling Light with Thomas Merton, Bashō, Edward Abbey, Annie Dillard & Others
by Philip Harnden
Invites you to consider a more graceful way of traveling through life. PB includes journal pages to help you get started on your own spiritual journey.
5 x 7¼, 144 pp, Quality PB, 978-1-59473-181-5 **$12.99**
5 x 7¼, 128 pp, HC, 978-1-893361-76-8 **$16.95**

Or phone, fax, mail or e-mail to: SKYLIGHT PATHS Publishing
Sunset Farm Offices, Route 4 • P.O. Box 237 • Woodstock, Vermont 05091
Tel: (802) 457-4000 • Fax: (802) 457-4004 • www.skylightpaths.com
Credit card orders: (800) 962-4544 (8:30AM–5:30PM EST Monday–Friday)
Generous discounts on quantity orders. SATISFACTION GUARANTEED. Prices subject to change.

Children's Spiritual Biography

Ten Amazing People
And How They Changed the World
by Maura D. Shaw; Foreword by Dr. Robert Coles
Full-color illus. by Stephen Marchesi

For ages 7 & up

Shows kids that spiritual people can have an exciting impact on the world around them. Kids will delight in reading about these amazing people and what they accomplished through their words and actions.

Black Elk • Dorothy Day • Malcolm X • Mahatma Gandhi • Martin Luther King, Jr. • Mother Teresa • Janusz Korczak • Desmond Tutu • Thich Nhat Hanh • Albert Schweitzer

"Best Juvenile/Young Adult Non-Fiction Book of the Year."
—*Independent Publisher*

"Will inspire adults and children alike."
—*Globe and Mail* (Toronto)

8½ x 11, 48 pp, Full-color illus., HC, 978-1-893361-47-8 **$17.95** *For ages 7 & up*

Spiritual Biographies for Young People
For Ages 7 & Up
By Maura D. Shaw; Illus. by Stephen Marchesi
6¾ x 8¾, 32 pp, Full-color and b/w illus., HC

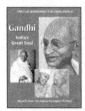
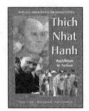

Black Elk: Native American Man of Spirit
Through historically accurate illustrations and photos, inspiring age-appropriate activities and Black Elk's own words, this colorful biography introduces children to a remarkable person who ensured that the traditions and beliefs of his people would not be forgotten.
978-1-59473-043-6 **$12.99**

Dorothy Day: A Catholic Life of Action
Introduces children to one of the most inspiring women of the twentieth century, a down-to-earth spiritual leader who saw the presence of God in every person she met. Includes practical activities, a timeline and a list of important words to know.
978-1-59473-011-5 **$12.99**

Gandhi: India's Great Soul
The only biography of Gandhi that balances a simple text with illustrations, photos and activities that encourage children and adults to talk about how to make changes happen without violence. Introduces children to important concepts of freedom, equality and justice among people of all backgrounds and religions.
978-1-893361-91-1 **$12.95**

Thich Nhat Hanh: Buddhism in Action
Warm illustrations, photos, age-appropriate activities and Thich Nhat Hanh's own poems introduce a great man to children in a way they can understand and enjoy. Includes a list of important Buddhist words to know.
978-1-893361-87-4 **$12.95**

Children's Spirituality

ENDORSED BY CATHOLIC, PROTESTANT, JEWISH, AND BUDDHIST RELIGIOUS LEADERS

Adam & Eve's First Sunset: God's New Day
by Sandy Eisenberg Sasso; Full-color illus. by Joani Keller Rothenberg 9 x 12, 32 pp, Full-color illus., HC, 978-1-58023-177-0 **$17.95*** *For ages 4 & up*

Because Nothing Looks Like God
by Lawrence Kushner and Karen Kushner; Full-color illus. by Dawn W. Majewski
Invites parents and children to explore the questions we all have about God.
11 x 8½, 32 pp, Full-color illus., HC, 978-1-58023-092-6 **$17.99*** *For ages 4 & up*

Also available: **Teacher's Guide** 8½ x 11, 22 pp, PB, 978-1-58023-140-4 **$6.95**

But God Remembered: Stories of Women from Creation to the Promised Land
by Sandy Eisenberg Sasso; Full-color illus. by Bethanne Andersen
A fascinating collection of four different stories of women only briefly mentioned in biblical tradition and religious texts.
9 x 12, 32 pp, Full-color illus., Quality PB, 978-1-58023-372-9 **$8.99*** *For ages 8 & up*

Cain & Abel: Finding the Fruits of Peace
by Sandy Eisenberg Sasso; Full-color illus. by Joani Keller Rothenberg
A sensitive recasting of the ancient tale shows we have the power to deal with anger in positive ways. "Editor's Choice." —American Library Association's *Booklist*
9 x 12, 32 pp, Full-color illus., HC, 978-1-58023-123-7 **$16.95*** *For ages 5 & up*

Does God Hear My Prayer?
by August Gold; Full-color photos by Diane Hardy Waller
Introduces preschoolers and young readers to prayer and how it helps them express their own emotions.
10 x 8½, 32 pp, Full-color photo illus., Quality PB, 978-1-59473-102-0 **$8.99** *For ages 3–6*

The 11th Commandment: Wisdom from Our Children *by The Children of America*
"If there were an Eleventh Commandment, what would it be?" Children of many religious denominations across America answer this question—in their own drawings and words. "A rare book of spiritual celebration for all people, of all ages, for all time." —*Bookviews* 8 x 10, 48 pp, Full-color illus., HC, 978-1-879045-46-0 **$16.95*** *For all ages*

For Heaven's Sake *by Sandy Eisenberg Sasso; Full-color illus. by Kathryn Kunz Finney*
Heaven is often found where you least expect it.
9 x 12, 32 pp, Full-color illus., HC, 978-1-58023-054-4 **$16.95*** *For ages 4 & up*

God in Between *by Sandy Eisenberg Sasso; Full-color illus. by Sally Sweetland*
A magical, mythical tale that teaches that God can be found where we are.
9 x 12, 32 pp, Full-color illus., HC, 978-1-879045-86-6 **$16.95*** *For ages 4 & up*

God's Paintbrush: Special 10th Anniversary Edition
by Sandy Eisenberg Sasso; Full-color illus. by Annette Compton
Invites children of all faiths and backgrounds to encounter God through moments in their own lives. 11 x 8½, 32 pp, Full-color illus., HC, 978-1-58023-195-4 **$17.95*** *For ages 4 & up*

Also available: **God's Paintbrush Teacher's Guide**
8½ x 11, 32 pp, PB, 978-1-879045-57-6 **$8.95**

God's Paintbrush Celebration Kit: A Spiritual Activity Kit for Teachers and Students of All Faiths, All Backgrounds 9½ x 12, 40 Full-color Activity Sheets & Teacher Folder w/ complete instructions, HC, 978-1-58023-050-6 **$21.95**
Additional activity sheets available:
8-Student Activity Sheet Pack (40 sheets/5 sessions), 978-1-58023-058-2 **$19.95**
Single-Student Activity Sheet Pack (5 sessions), 978-1-58023-059-9 **$3.95**

I Am God's Paintbrush (A Board Book)
by Sandy Eisenberg Sasso; Full-color illus. by Annette Compton
5 x 5, 24 pp, Full-color illus., Board Book, 978-1-59473-265-2 **$7.99** *For ages 0–4*

* A book from Jewish Lights, SkyLight Paths' sister imprint

Children's Spirituality

Remembering My Grandparent: A Kid's Own Grief Workbook in the Christian Tradition *by Nechama Liss-Levinson, PhD, and Rev. Molly Phinney Baskette, MDiv* 8 x 10, 48 pp, 2-color text, HC, 978-1-59473-212-6 **$16.99** *For ages 7 & up*

Does God Ever Sleep? *by Joan Sauro, CSJ*
A charming nighttime reminder that God is always present in our lives.
10 x 8¼, 32 pp, Full-color photos, Quality PB, 978-1-59473-110-5 **$8.99** *For ages 3–6*

Does God Forgive Me? *by August Gold; Full-color photos by Diane Hardy Waller*
Gently shows how God forgives all that we do if we are truly sorry.
10 x 8¼, 32 pp, Full-color photos, Quality PB, 978-1-59473-142-6 **$8.99** *For ages 3–6*

God Said Amen *by Sandy Eisenberg Sasso; Full-color illus. by Avi Katz*
A warm and inspiring tale that shows us that we need only reach out to each other to find the answers to our prayers.
9 x 12, 32 pp, Full-color illus., HC, 978-1-58023-080-3 **$16.95*** *For ages 4 & up*

How Does God Listen? *by Kay Lindahl; Full-color photos by Cynthia Maloney*
How do we know when God is listening to us? Children will find the answers to these questions as they engage their senses while the story unfolds, learning how God listens in the wind, waves, clouds, hot chocolate, perfume, our tears and our laughter.
10 x 8¼, 32 pp, Full-color photos, Quality PB, 978-1-59473-084-9 **$8.99** *For ages 3–6*

In God's Hands *by Lawrence Kushner and Gary Schmidt; Full-color illus. by Matthew J. Baek*
9 x 12, 32 pp, Full-color illus., HC, 978-1-58023-224-1 **$16.99*** *For ages 5 & up*

In God's Name *by Sandy Eisenberg Sasso; Full-color illus. by Phoebe Stone*
Like an ancient myth in its poetic text and vibrant illustrations, this award-winning modern fable about the search for God's name celebrates the diversity and, at the same time, the unity of all the people of the world.
9 x 12, 32 pp, Full-color illus., HC, 978-1-879045-26-2 **$16.99*** *For ages 4 & up*

Also available in Spanish: **El nombre de Dios**
9 x 12, 32 pp, Full-color illus., HC, 978-1-893361-63-8 **$16.95**

In Our Image: God's First Creatures
by Nancy Sohn Swartz; Full-color illus. by Melanie Hall
A playful new twist on the Genesis story—from the perspective of the animals. Celebrates the interconnectedness of nature and the harmony of all living things.
9 x 12, 32 pp, Full-color illus., HC, 978-1-879045-99-6 **$16.95*** *For ages 4 & up*

Noah's Wife: The Story of Naamah
by Sandy Eisenberg Sasso; Full-color illus. by Bethanne Andersen
Opens young readers' religious imaginations to new ideas about the well-known story of the Flood. When God tells Noah to bring the animals of the world onto the ark, God also calls on Naamah, Noah's wife, to save each plant on Earth.
9 x 12, 32 pp, Full-color illus., HC, 978-1-58023-134-3 **$16.95*** *For ages 4 & up*

Also available: **Naamah:** Noah's Wife (A Board Book)
by Sandy Eisenberg Sasso; Full-color illus. by Bethanne Andersen
5 x 5, 24 pp, Full-color illus., Board Book, 978-1-893361-56-0 **$7.95** *For ages 0–4*

Where Does God Live? *by August Gold and Matthew J. Perlman*
Helps children and their parents find God in the world around us with simple, practical examples children can relate to.
10 x 8¼, 32 pp, Full-color photos, Quality PB, 978-1-893361-39-3 **$8.99** *For ages 3–6*

* A book from Jewish Lights, SkyLight Paths' sister imprint

Children's Spirituality—Board Books

Adam & Eve's New Day
by Sandy Eisenberg Sasso; Full-color illus. by Joani Keller Rothenberg
A lesson in hope for every child who has worried about what comes next. Abridged from *Adam & Eve's First Sunset*.
5 x 5, 24 pp, Full-color illus., Board Book, 978-1-59473-205-8 **$7.99** *For ages 0–4*

How Did the Animals Help God?
by Nancy Sohn Swartz; Full-color illus. by Melanie Hall
God asks all of nature to offer gifts to humankind—with a promise that they will care for creation in return. Abridged from *In Our Image*.
5 x 5, 24 pp, Full-color illus., Board Book, 978-1-59473-044-3 **$7.99** *For ages 0–4*

How Does God Make Things Happen?
by Lawrence and Karen Kushner; Full-color illus. by Dawn W. Majewski
A charming invitation for young children to explore how God makes things happen in our world. Abridged from *Because Nothing Looks Like God*.
5 x 5, 24 pp, Full-color illus., Board Book, 978-1-893361-24-9 **$7.95** *For ages 0–4*

What Does God Look Like?
by Lawrence and Karen Kushner; Full-color illus. by Dawn W. Majewski
A simple way for young children to explore the ways that we "see" God. Abridged from *Because Nothing Looks Like God*.
5 x 5, 24 pp, Full-color illus., Board Book, 978-1-893361-23-2 **$7.99** *For ages 0–4*

What Is God's Name?
by Sandy Eisenberg Sasso; Full-color illus. by Phoebe Stone
Everyone and everything in the world has a name. What is God's name? Abridged from the award-winning *In God's Name*.
5 x 5, 24 pp, Full-color illus., Board Book, 978-1-893361-10-2 **$7.99** *For ages 0–4*

Where Is God? *by Lawrence and Karen Kushner; Full-color illus. by Dawn W. Majewski* A gentle way for young children to explore how God is with us every day, in every way. Abridged from *Because Nothing Looks Like God*.
5 x 5, 24 pp, Full-color illus., Board Book, 978-1-893361-17-1 **$7.99** *For ages 0–4*

What You Will See Inside ...

Fun-to-read books with vibrant full-color photos show children ages 6 and up the who, what, when, where, why and how of traditional houses of worship, liturgical celebrations and rituals of different world faiths, empowering them to respect and understand their own religious traditions—and those of their friends and neighbors.

What You Will See Inside a Catholic Church
by Rev. Michael Keane; Foreword by Robert J. Kealey, EdD
Full-color photos by Aaron Pepis
8½ x 10¼, 32 pp, Full-color photos, HC, 978-1-893361-54-6 **$17.95**

Also available in Spanish: **Lo que se puede ver dentro de una iglesia católica**
8½ x 10¼, 32 pp, Full-color photos, HC, 978-1-893361-66-9 **$16.95**

What You Will See Inside a Hindu Temple
by Mahendra Jani, PhD, and Vandana Jani, PhD; Full-color photos by Neirah Bhargava and Vijay Dave
8½ x 10¼, 32 pp, Full-color photos, HC, 978-1-59473-116-7 **$17.99**

What You Will See Inside a Mosque
by Aisha Karen Khan; Full-color photos by Aaron Pepis
8½ x 10¼, 32 pp, Full-color photos, Quality PB, 978-1-59473-257-7 **$8.99**

What You Will See Inside a Synagogue
by Rabbi Lawrence A. Hoffman, PhD, and Dr. Ron Wolfson; Full-color photos by Bill Aron
8½ x 10¼, 32 pp, Full-color photos, Quality PB, 978-1-59473-256-0 **$8.99**

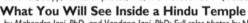

Bible Stories / Folktales

Abraham's Bind & Other Bible Tales of Trickery, Folly, Mercy and Love by Michael J. Caduto
New retellings of episodes in the lives of familiar biblical characters explore relevant life lessons. 6 x 9, 224 pp, HC, 978-1-59473-186-0 **$19.99**

Daughters of the Desert: Stories of Remarkable Women from Christian, Jewish and Muslim Traditions by Claire Rudolf Murphy,
Meghan Nuttall Sayres, Mary Cronk Farrell, Sarah Conover and Betsy Wharton
Breathes new life into the old tales of our female ancestors in faith. Uses traditional scriptural passages as starting points, then with vivid detail fills in historical context and place. Chapters reveal the voices of Sarah, Hagar, Huldah, Esther, Salome, Mary Magdalene, Lydia, Khadija, Fatima and many more. Historical fiction ideal for readers of all ages.
5½ x 8½, 192 pp, Quality PB, 978-1-59473-106-8 **$14.99** Inc. reader's discussion guide
HC, 978-1-893361-72-0 **$19.95**

The Triumph of Eve & Other Subversive Bible Tales
by Matt Biers-Ariel
These engaging retellings of familiar Bible stories are witty, often hilarious and always profound. They invite you to grapple with questions and issues that are often hidden in the original texts.
5½ x 8½, 192 pp, Quality PB, 978-1-59473-176-1 **$14.99**
Also available: **The Triumph of Eve Teacher's Guide**
8½ x 11, 44 pp, PB, 978-1-59473-152-5 **$8.99**

Wisdom in the Telling
Finding Inspiration and Grace in Traditional Folktales and Myths Retold
by Lorraine Hartin-Gelardi
6 x 9, 192 pp, HC, 978-1-59473-185-3 **$19.99**

Religious Etiquette / Reference

How to Be a Perfect Stranger, 5th Edition: The Essential Religious Etiquette Handbook Edited by Stuart M. Matlins and Arthur J. Magida

The indispensable guidebook to help the well-meaning guest when visiting other people's religious ceremonies. A straightforward guide to the rituals and celebrations of the major religions and denominations in the United States and Canada from the perspective of an interested guest of any other faith, based on information obtained from authorities of each religion. Belongs in every living room, library and office. Covers:
African American Methodist Churches • Assemblies of God • Bahá'í Faith • Baptist • Buddhist • Christian Church (Disciples of Christ) • Christian Science (Church of Christ, Scientist) • Churches of Christ • Episcopalian and Anglican • Hindu • Islam • Jehovah's Witnesses • Jewish • Lutheran • Mennonite/Amish • Methodist • Mormon (Church of Jesus Christ of Latter-day Saints) • Native American/First Nations • Orthodox Churches • Pentecostal Church of God • Presbyterian • Quaker (Religious Society of Friends) • Reformed Church in America/Canada • Roman Catholic • Seventh-day Adventist • Sikh • Unitarian Universalist • United Church of Canada • United Church of Christ

"The things Miss Manners forgot to tell us about religion."

—*Los Angeles Times*

"Finally, for those inclined to undertake their own spiritual journeys ... tells visitors what to expect." —*New York Times*

6 x 9, 432 pp, Quality PB, 978-1-59473-294-2 **$19.99**

The Perfect Stranger's Guide to Funerals and Grieving Practices: A Guide to Etiquette in Other People's Religious Ceremonies Edited by Stuart M. Matlins
6 x 9, 240 pp, Quality PB, 978-1-893361-20-1 **$16.95**

The Perfect Stranger's Guide to Wedding Ceremonies: A Guide to Etiquette in Other People's Religious Ceremonies Edited by Stuart M. Matlins
6 x 9, 208 pp, Quality PB, 978-1-893361-19-5 **$16.95**

Spirituality

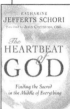

The Heartbeat of God: Finding the Sacred in the Middle of Everything
by Katharine Jefferts Schori; Foreword by Joan Chittister, OSB
Explores our connections to other people, to other nations and with the environment through the lens of faith. 6 x 9, 240 pp, HC, 978-1-59473-292-8 **$21.99**

A Dangerous Dozen: Twelve Christians Who Threatened the Status Quo but Taught Us to Live Like Jesus
by the Rev. Canon C. K. Robertson, PhD; Foreword by Archbishop Desmond Tutu
Profiles twelve visionary men and women who challenged society and showed the world a different way of living. 6 x 9, 208 pp, Quality PB, 978-1-59473-298-0 **$16.99**

Decision Making & Spiritual Discernment: The Sacred Art of Finding Your Way *by Nancy L. Bieber*
Presents three essential aspects of Spirit-led decision making: willingness, attentiveness and responsiveness. 5½ x 8½, 208 pp, Quality PB, 978-1-59473-289-8 **$16.99**

Laugh Your Way to Grace: Reclaiming the Spiritual Power of Humor
by Rev. Susan Sparks A powerful, humorous case for laughter as a spiritual, healing path. 6 x 9, 176 pp, Quality PB, 978-1-59473-280-5 **$16.99**

Living into Hope: A Call to Spiritual Action for Such a Time as This
by Rev. Dr. Joan Brown Campbell; Foreword by Karen Armstrong
A visionary minister speaks out on the pressing issues that face us today, offering

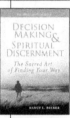

inspiration and challenge. 6 x 9, 208 pp, HC, 978-1-59473-283-6 **$21.99**

Claiming Earth as Common Ground: The Ecological Crisis through the Lens of Faith
by Andrea Cohen-Kiener; Foreword by Rev. Sally Bingham
6 x 9, 192 pp, Quality PB, 978-1-59473-261-4 **$16.99**

Bread, Body, Spirit: Finding the Sacred in Food
Edited and with Introductions by Alice Peck 6 x 9, 224 pp, Quality PB, 978-1-59473-242-3 **$19.99**

Creating a Spiritual Retirement: A Guide to the Unseen Possibilities in Our Lives
by Molly Srode 6 x 9, 208 pp, b/w photos, Quality PB, 978-1-59473-050-4 **$14.99**

Creative Aging: Rethinking Retirement and Non-Retirement in a Changing World
by Marjory Zoet Bankson 6 x 9, 160 pp, Quality PB, 978-1-59473-281-2 **$16.99**

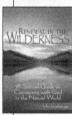

Keeping Spiritual Balance as We Grow Older: More than 65 Creative Ways to Use Purpose, Prayer, and the Power of Spirit to Build a Meaningful Retirement
by Molly and Bernie Srode 8 x 8, 224 pp, Quality PB, 978-1-59473-042-9 **$16.99**

Hearing the Call across Traditions: Readings on Faith and Service
Edited by Adam Davis; Foreword by Eboo Patel
6 x 9, 352 pp, Quality PB, 978-1-59473-303-1 **$18.99**; HC, 978-1-59473-264-5 **$29.99**

Honoring Motherhood: Prayers, Ceremonies & Blessings
Edited and with Introductions by Lynn L. Caruso 5 x 7¼, 272 pp, HC, 978-1-59473-239-3 **$19.99**

Journeys of Simplicity: Traveling Light with Thomas Merton, Bashō, Edward Abbey, Annie Dillard & Others *by Philip Harnden*
5 x 7¼, 144 pp, Quality PB, 978-1-59473-181-5 **$12.99**; 128 pp, HC, 978-1-893361-76-8 **$16.95**

The Losses of Our Lives: The Sacred Gifts of Renewal in Everyday Loss
by Dr. Nancy Copeland-Payton 6 x 9, 192 pp, HC, 978-1-59473-271-3 **$19.99**

Renewal in the Wilderness: A Spiritual Guide to Connecting with God in the Natural World *by John Lionberger*
6 x 9, 176 pp, b/w photos, Quality PB, 978-1-59473-219-5 **$16.99**

Soul Fire: Accessing Your Creativity
by Thomas Ryan, CSP 6 x 9, 160 pp, Quality PB, 978-1-59473-243-0 **$16.99**

A Spirituality for Brokenness: Discovering Your Deepest Self in Difficult Times
by Terry Taylor 6 x 9, 176 pp, Quality PB, 978-1-59473-229-4 **$16.99**

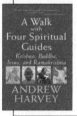

A Walk with Four Spiritual Guides: Krishna, Buddha, Jesus, and Ramakrishna
by Andrew Harvey 5½ x 8½, 192 pp, b/w photos & illus., Quality PB, 978-1-59473-138-9 **$15.99**

The Workplace and Spirituality: New Perspectives on Research and Practice
Edited by Dr. Joan Marques, Dr. Satinder Dhiman and Dr. Richard King
6 x 9, 256 pp, HC, 978-1-59473-260-7 **$29.99**

Spirituality of the Seasons

Autumn: A Spiritual Biography of the Season
Edited by Gary Schmidt and Susan M. Felch; Illus. by Mary Azarian
Rejoice in autumn as a time of preparation and reflection. Includes Wendell Berry, David James Duncan, Robert Frost, A. Bartlett Giamatti, E. B. White, P. D. James, Julian of Norwich, Garret Keizer, Tracy Kidder, Anne Lamott, May Sarton.
6 x 9, 320 pp, b/w illus., Quality PB, 978-1-59473-118-1 **$18.99**

Spring: A Spiritual Biography of the Season
Edited by Gary Schmidt and Susan M. Felch; Illus. by Mary Azarian
Explore the gentle unfurling of spring and reflect on how nature celebrates rebirth and renewal. Includes Jane Kenyon, Lucy Larcom, Harry Thurston, Nathaniel Hawthorne, Noel Perrin, Annie Dillard, Martha Ballard, Barbara Kingsolver, Dorothy Wordsworth, Donald Hall, David Brill, Lionel Basney, Isak Dinesen, Paul Laurence Dunbar. 6 x 9, 352 pp, b/w illus., Quality PB, 978-1-59473-246-1 **$18.99**

Summer: A Spiritual Biography of the Season
Edited by Gary Schmidt and Susan M. Felch; Illus. by Barry Moser
"A sumptuous banquet.... These selections lift up an exquisite wholeness found within an everyday sophistication." — ★ *Publishers Weekly* starred review
Includes Anne Lamott, Luci Shaw, Ray Bradbury, Richard Selzer, Thomas Lynch, Walt Whitman, Carl Sandburg, Sherman Alexie, Madeleine L'Engle, Jamaica Kincaid.
6 x 9, 304 pp, b/w illus., Quality PB, 978-1-59473-183-9 **$18.99**
HC, 978-1-59473-083-2 **$21.99**

Winter: A Spiritual Biography of the Season
Edited by Gary Schmidt and Susan M. Felch; Illus. by Barry Moser
"This outstanding anthology features top-flight nature and spirituality writers on the fierce, inexorable season of winter.... Remarkably lively and warm, despite the icy subject." — ★ *Publishers Weekly* starred review
Includes Will Campbell, Rachel Carson, Annie Dillard, Donald Hall, Ron Hansen, Jane Kenyon, Jamaica Kincaid, Barry Lopez, Kathleen Norris, John Updike, E. B. White.
6 x 9, 288 pp, b/w illus., Deluxe PB w/ flaps, 978-1-893361-92-8 **$18.95**
HC, 978-1-893361-53-9 **$21.95**

Spirituality / Animal Companions

Blessing the Animals: Prayers and Ceremonies to Celebrate God's Creatures, Wild and Tame *Edited and with Introductions by Lynn L. Caruso*
5¼ x 7¼, 256 pp, Quality PB, 978-1-59473-253-9 **$15.99**; HC, 978-1-59473-145-7 **$19.99**

Remembering My Pet: A Kid's Own Spiritual Workbook for When a Pet Dies
by Nechama Liss-Levinson, PhD, and Rev. Molly Phinney Baskette, MDiv; Foreword by Lynn L. Caruso
8 x 10, 48 pp, 2-color text, HC, 978-1-59473-221-8 **$16.99**

What Animals Can Teach Us about Spirituality: Inspiring Lessons from Wild and Tame Creatures *by Diana L. Guerrero* 6 x 9, 176 pp, Quality PB, 978-1-893361-84-3 **$16.95**

Spirituality—A Week Inside

Lighting the Lamp of Wisdom: A Week Inside a Yoga Ashram
by John Ittner; Foreword by Dr. David Frawley
6 x 9, 192 pp, b/w photos, Quality PB, 978-1-893361-52-2 **$15.95**

Making a Heart for God: A Week Inside a Catholic Monastery
by Dianne Aprile; Foreword by Brother Patrick Hart, OCSO
6 x 9, 224 pp, b/w photos, Quality PB, 978-1-893361-49-2 **$16.95**

Waking Up: A Week Inside a Zen Monastery
by Jack Maguire; Foreword by John Daido Loori, Roshi
6 x 9, 224 pp, b/w photos, Quality PB, 978-1-893361-55-3 **$16.95**; HC, 978-1-893361-13-3 **$21.95**

Spiritual Poetry—The Mystic Poets

Experience these mystic poets as you never have before. Each beautiful, compact book includes a brief introduction to the poet's time and place, a summary of the major themes of the poet's mysticism and religious tradition, essential selections from the poet's most important works, and an appreciative preface by a contemporary spiritual writer.

Hafiz
The Mystic Poets
Translated and with Notes by Gertrude Bell
Preface by Ibrahim Gamard
Hafiz is known throughout the world as Persia's greatest poet, with sales of his poems in Iran today only surpassed by those of the Qur'an itself. His probing and joyful verse speaks to people from all backgrounds who long to taste and feel divine love and experience harmony with all living things.
5 x 7¼, 144 pp, HC, 978-1-59473-009-2 **$16.99**

Hopkins
The Mystic Poets
Preface by Rev. Thomas Ryan, CSP
Gerard Manley Hopkins, Christian mystical poet, is beloved for his use of fresh language and startling metaphors to describe the world around him. Although his verse is lovely, beneath the surface lies a searching soul, wrestling with and yearning for God.
5 x 7¼, 112 pp, HC, 978-1-59473-010-8 **$16.99**

Tagore
The Mystic Poets
Preface by Swami Adiswarananda
Rabindranath Tagore is often considered the Shakespeare of modern India. A great mystic, Tagore was the teacher of W. B. Yeats and Robert Frost, the close friend of Albert Einstein and Mahatma Gandhi, and the winner of the Nobel Prize for Literature. This beautiful sampling of Tagore's two most important works, *The Gardener* and *Gitanjali,* offers a glimpse into his spiritual vision that has inspired people around the world.
5 x 7¼, 144 pp, HC, 978-1-59473-008-5 **$16.99**

Whitman
The Mystic Poets
Preface by Gary David Comstock
Walt Whitman was the most innovative and influential poet of the nineteenth century. This beautiful sampling of Whitman's most important poetry from *Leaves of Grass,* and selections from his prose writings, offers a glimpse into the spiritual side of his most radical themes—love for country, love for others and love of self.
5 x 7¼, 192 pp, HC, 978-1-59473-041-2 **$16.99**

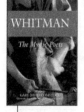

Women's Interest

Women, Spirituality and Transformative Leadership
Where Grace Meets Power
Edited by Kathe Schaaf, Kay Lindahl, Kathleen S. Hurty, PhD, and Reverend Guo Cheen
A dynamic conversation on the power of women's spiritual leadership and its emerging patterns of transformation.
6 x 9, 288 pp, Hardcover, 978-1-59473-313-0 **$24.99**

Spiritually Healthy Divorce: Navigating Disruption with Insight & Hope
by Carolyne Call A spiritual map to help you move through the twists and turns of divorce. 6 x 9, 224 pp, Quality PB, 978-1-59473-288-1 **$16.99**

New Feminist Christianity: Many Voices, Many Views
Edited by Mary E. Hunt and Diann L. Neu
Insights from ministers and theologians, activists and leaders, artists and liturgists who are shaping the future. Taken together, their voices offer a starting point for building new models of religious life and worship.
6 x 9, 384 pp, HC, 978-1-59473-285-0 **$24.99**

New Jewish Feminism: Probing the Past, Forging the Future
Edited by Rabbi Elyse Goldstein; Foreword by Anita Diamant
Looks at the growth and accomplishments of Jewish feminism and what they mean for Jewish women today and tomorrow. Features the voices of women from every area of Jewish life, addressing the important issues that concern Jewish women.
6 x 9, 480 pp, Quality PB, 978-1-58023-448-1 **$19.99**; HC, 978-1-58023-359-0 **$24.99***

Bread, Body, Spirit: Finding the Sacred in Food
Edited and with Introductions by Alice Peck 6 x 9, 224 pp, Quality PB, 978-1-59473-242-3 **$19.99**

Dance—The Sacred Art: The Joy of Movement as a Spiritual Practice
by Cynthia Winton-Henry 5½ x 8½, 224 pp, Quality PB, 978-1-59473-268-3 **$16.99**

Daughters of the Desert: Stories of Remarkable Women from Christian, Jewish and Muslim Traditions
by Claire Rudolf Murphy, Meghan Nuttall Sayres, Mary Cronk Farrell, Sarah Conover and Betsy Wharton
5½ x 8½, 192 pp, Illus., Quality PB, 978-1-59473-106-8 **$14.99** Inc. reader's discussion guide

The Divine Feminine in Biblical Wisdom Literature
Selections Annotated & Explained
Translation & Annotation by Rabbi Rami Shapiro; Foreword by Rev. Cynthia Bourgeault, PhD
5½ x 8½, 240 pp, Quality PB, 978-1-59473-109-9 **$16.99**

Divining the Body: Reclaim the Holiness of Your Physical Self
by Jan Phillips 8 x 8, 256 pp, Quality PB, 978-1-59473-080-1 **$16.99**

Honoring Motherhood: Prayers, Ceremonies & Blessings
Edited and with Introductions by Lynn L. Caruso 5 x 7¼, 272 pp, HC, 978-1-59473-239-3 **$19.99**

Next to Godliness: Finding the Sacred in Housekeeping
Edited by Alice Peck 6 x 9, 224 pp, Quality PB, 978-1-59473-214-0 **$19.99**

ReVisions: Seeing Torah through a Feminist Lens
by Rabbi Elyse Goldstein 5½ x 8½, 224 pp, Quality PB, 978-1-58023-117-6 **$16.95***

The Triumph of Eve & Other Subversive Bible Tales
by Matt Biers-Ariel 5½ x 8½, 192 pp, Quality PB, 978-1-59473-176-1 **$14.99**

White Fire: A Portrait of Women Spiritual Leaders in America
by Malka Drucker; Photos by Gay Block 7 x 10, 320 pp, b/w photos, HC, 978-1-893361-64-5 **$24.95**

Woman Spirit Awakening in Nature: Growing Into the Fullness of Who You Are
by Nancy Barrett Chickerneo, PhD; Foreword by Eileen Fisher
8 x 8, 224 pp, b/w illus., Quality PB, 978-1-59473-250-8 **$16.99**

Women of Color Pray: Voices of Strength, Faith, Healing, Hope and Courage
Edited and with Introductions by Christal M. Jackson
5 x 7¼, 208 pp, Quality PB, 978-1-59473-077-1 **$15.99**

The Women's Torah Commentary: New Insights from Women Rabbis on the 54 Weekly Torah Portions *Edited by Rabbi Elyse Goldstein*
6 x 9, 496 pp, Quality PB, 978-1-58023-370-5 **$19.99**; HC, 978-1-58023-076-6 **$34.95***

* A book from Jewish Lights, SkyLight Paths' sister imprint

Spirituality & Crafts

Beading—The Creative Spirit: Finding Your Sacred Center through the Art of Beadwork *by Rev. Wendy Ellsworth*
Invites you on a spiritual pilgrimage into the kaleidoscope world of glass and color. 7 x 9, 240 pp, 8-page color insert, 40+ b/w photos and 40 diagrams, Quality PB, 978-1-59473-267-6 **$18.99**

Contemplative Crochet: A Hands-On Guide for Interlocking Faith and Craft *by Cindy Crandall-Frazier; Foreword by Linda Skolnik*
Illuminates the spiritual lessons you can learn through crocheting.
7 x 9, 208 pp, b/w photos, Quality PB, 978-1-59473-238-6 **$16.99**

The Knitting Way: A Guide to Spiritual Self-Discovery
by Linda Skolnik and Janice MacDaniels Examines how you can explore and strengthen your spiritual life through knitting.
7 x 9, 240 pp, b/w photos, Quality PB, 978-1-59473-079-5 **$16.99**

The Painting Path: Embodying Spiritual Discovery through Yoga, Brush and Color *by Linda Novick; Foreword by Richard Segalman*
Explores the divine connection you can experience through art.
7 x 9, 208 pp, 8-page color insert, plus b/w photos,
Quality PB, 978-1-59473-226-3 **$18.99**

The Quilting Path: A Guide to Spiritual Discovery through Fabric, Thread and Kabbalah *by Louise Silk*
Explores how to cultivate personal growth through quilt making.
7 x 9, 192 pp, b/w photos and illus., Quality PB, 978-1-59473-206-5 **$16.99**

The Scrapbooking Journey: A Hands-On Guide to Spiritual Discovery *by Cory Richardson-Lauve; Foreword by Stacy Julian* Reveals how this craft can become a practice used to deepen and shape your life.
7 x 9, 176 pp, 8-page color insert, plus b/w photos, Quality PB, 978-1-59473-216-4 **$18.99**

The Soulwork of Clay: A Hands-On Approach to Spirituality
by Marjory Zoet Bankson; Photos by Peter Bankson
Takes you through the seven-step process of making clay into a pot, drawing parallels at each stage to the process of spiritual growth.
7 x 9, 192 pp, b/w photos, Quality PB, 978-1-59473-249-2 **$16.99**

Kabbalah / Enneagram
(Books from Jewish Lights Publishing, SkyLight Paths' sister imprint)

Cast in God's Image: Discover Your Personality Type Using the Enneagram and Kabbalah *by Rabbi Howard A. Addison, PhD* 7 x 9, 176 pp, Quality PB, 978-1-58023-124-4 **$16.95**

Ehyeh: A Kabbalah for Tomorrow *by Rabbi Arthur Green, PhD*
6 x 9, 224 pp, Quality PB, 978-1-58023-213-5 **$18.99**

The Enneagram and Kabbalah, 2nd Edition: Reading Your Soul
by Rabbi Howard A. Addison, PhD 6 x 9, 192 pp, Quality PB, 978-1-58023-229-6 **$16.99**

The Gift of Kabbalah: Discovering the Secrets of Heaven, Renewing Your Life on Earth *by Tamar Frankiel, PhD* 6 x 9, 256 pp, Quality PB, 978-1-58023-141-1 **$16.95**

God in Your Body: Kabbalah, Mindfulness and Embodied Spiritual Practice
by Jay Michaelson 6 x 9, 272 pp, Quality PB, 978-1-58023-304-0 **$18.99**

Jewish Mysticism and the Spiritual Life: Classical Texts, Contemporary Reflections
Edited by Dr. Lawrence Fine, Dr. Eitan Fishbane and Rabbi Or N. Rose
6 x 9, 256 pp, HC, 978-1-58023-434-4 **$24.99**

Kabbalah: A Brief Introduction for Christians
by Tamar Frankiel, PhD 5½ x 8½, 208 pp, Quality PB, 978-1-58023-303-3 **$16.99**

Zohar: Annotated & Explained *Translation & Annotation by Daniel C. Matt;*
Foreword by Andrew Harvey 5½ x 8½, 176 pp, Quality PB, 978-1-893361-51-5 **$15.99**

Spiritual Practice

Fly Fishing—The Sacred Art: Casting a Fly as a Spiritual Practice
by Rabbi Eric Eisenkramer and Rev. Michael Attas, MD
Illuminates what fly fishing can teach you about reflection, awe and wonder; the
benefits of solitude; the blessing of community and the search for the Divine.
5½ x 8½, 192 pp (est), Quality PB, 978-1-59473-299-7 **$16.99**

***Lectio Divina*—The Sacred Art:** Transforming Words & Images into
Heart-Centered Prayer *by Christine Valters Paintner, PhD*
Expands the practice of sacred reading beyond scriptural texts and makes it
accessible in contemporary life. 5½ x 8½, 240 pp, Quality PB, 978-1-59473-300-0 **$16.99**

Haiku—The Sacred Art: A Spiritual Practice in Three Lines
by Margaret D. McGee 5½ x 8½, 192 pp, Quality PB, 978-1-59473-269-0 **$16.99**

Dance—The Sacred Art: The Joy of Movement as a Spiritual Practice
by Cynthia Winton-Henry 5½ x 8½, 224 pp, Quality PB, 978-1-59473-268-3 **$16.99**

Spiritual Adventures in the Snow: Skiing & Snowboarding as Renewal for Your Soul
by Dr. Marcia McFee and Rev. Karen Foster; Foreword by Paul Arthur
5½ x 8½, 208 pp, Quality PB, 978-1-59473-270-6 **$16.99**

Divining the Body: Reclaim the Holiness of Your Physical Self *by Jan Phillips*
8 x 8, 256 pp, Quality PB, 978-1-59473-080-1 **$16.99**

Everyday Herbs in Spiritual Life: A Guide to Many Practices
by Michael J. Caduto; Foreword by Rosemary Gladstar
7 x 9, 208 pp, 20+ b/w illus., Quality PB, 978-1-59473-174-7 **$16.99**

Giving—The Sacred Art: Creating a Lifestyle of Generosity
by Lauren Tyler Wright 5½ x 8½, 208 pp, Quality PB, 978-1-59473-224-9 **$16.99**

Hospitality—The Sacred Art: Discovering the Hidden Spiritual Power of Invitation
and Welcome *by Rev. Nanette Sawyer; Foreword by Rev. Dirk Ficca*
5½ x 8½, 208 pp, Quality PB, 978-1-59473-228-7 **$16.99**

Labyrinths from the Outside In: Walking to Spiritual Insight—A Beginner's Guide
by Donna Schaper and Carole Ann Camp
6 x 9, 208 pp, b/w illus. and photos, Quality PB, 978-1-893361-18-8 **$16.95**

Practicing the Sacred Art of Listening: A Guide to Enrich Your Relationships
and Kindle Your Spiritual Life *by Kay Lindahl* 8 x 8, 176 pp, Quality PB, 978-1-893361-85-0 **$16.95**

Recovery—The Sacred Art: The Twelve Steps as Spiritual Practice *by Rami Shapiro;
Foreword by Joan Borysenko, PhD* 5½ x 8½, 240 pp, Quality PB, 978-1-59473-259-1 **$16.99**

Running—The Sacred Art: Preparing to Practice *by Dr. Warren A. Kay; Foreword by
Kristin Armstrong* 5½ x 8½, 160 pp, Quality PB, 978-1-59473-227-0 **$16.99**

The Sacred Art of Chant: Preparing to Practice
by Ana Hernández 5½ x 8½, 192 pp, Quality PB, 978-1-59473-036-8 **$15.99**

The Sacred Art of Fasting: Preparing to Practice
by Thomas Ryan, CSP 5½ x 8½, 192 pp, Quality PB, 978-1-59473-078-8 **$15.99**

The Sacred Art of Forgiveness: Forgiving Ourselves and Others through God's Grace
by Marcia Ford 8 x 8, 176 pp, Quality PB, 978-1-59473-175-4 **$18.99**

The Sacred Art of Listening: Forty Reflections for Cultivating a Spiritual Practice
by Kay Lindahl; Illus. by Amy Schnapper 8 x 8, 160 pp, b/w illus., Quality PB, 978-1-893361-44-7 **$16.99**

The Sacred Art of Lovingkindness: Preparing to Practice
by Rabbi Rami Shapiro; Foreword by Marcia Ford 5½ x 8½, 176 pp, Quality PB, 978-1-59473-151-8 **$16.99**

Sacred Attention: A Spiritual Practice for Finding God in the Moment
by Margaret D. McGee 6 x 9, 144 pp, Quality PB, 978-1-59473-291-1 **$16.99**

Soul Fire: Accessing Your Creativity
by Thomas Ryan, CSP 6 x 9, 160 pp, Quality PB, 978-1-59473-243-0 **$16.99**

Thanking & Blessing—The Sacred Art: Spiritual Vitality through Gratefulness
by Jay Marshall, PhD; Foreword by Philip Gulley 5½ x 8½, 176 pp, Quality PB, 978-1-59473-231-7
$16.99

About SKYLIGHT PATHS Publishing

SkyLight Paths Publishing is creating a place where people of different spiritual traditions come together for challenge and inspiration, a place where we can help each other understand the mystery that lies at the heart of our existence.

Through spirituality, our religious beliefs are increasingly becoming a part of our lives—rather than *apart* from our lives. While many of us may be more interested than ever in spiritual growth, we may be less firmly planted in traditional religion. Yet, we do want to deepen our relationship to the sacred, to learn from our own as well as from other faith traditions, and to practice in new ways.

SkyLight Paths sees both believers and seekers as a community that increasingly transcends traditional boundaries of religion and denomination—people wanting to learn from each other, *walking together, finding the way.*

For your information and convenience, at the back of this book we have provided a list of other SkyLight Paths books you might find interesting and useful. They cover the following subjects:

Buddhism / Zen	Global Spiritual	Monasticism
Catholicism	Perspectives	Mysticism
Children's Books	Gnosticism	Poetry
Christianity	Hinduism /	Prayer
Comparative	Vedanta	Religious Etiquette
Religion	Inspiration	Retirement
Current Events	Islam / Sufism	Spiritual Biography
Earth-Based	Judaism	Spiritual Direction
Spirituality	Kabbalah	Spirituality
Enneagram	Meditation	Women's Interest
	Midrash Fiction	Worship

Or phone, fax, mail or e-mail to: SKYLIGHT PATHS Publishing
Sunset Farm Offices, Route 4 • P.O. Box 237 • Woodstock, Vermont 05091
Tel: (802) 457-4000 • Fax: (802) 457-4004 • www.skylightpaths.com
Credit card orders: (800) 962-4544 (8:30AM–5:30PM EST Monday–Friday)
Generous discounts on quantity orders. SATISFACTION GUARANTEED. Prices subject to change.

CPSIA information can be obtained
at www.ICGtesting.com
Printed in the USA
LVHW091800141119
637372LV00005B/914/P